Becoming a Writer

DOROTHEA BRANDE

Becoming a Writer

Foreword by
Malcolm Bradbury

MACMILLAN

First published in the United Kingdom 1983 by Papermac

Reissued 1996 by Macmillan Reference Books
an imprint of Macmillan Publishers Ltd
25 Eccleston Place, London SW1W 9NF
and Basingstoke

Associated companies throughout the world

ISBN 0 333 65377 7

8 9 7

A CIP catalogue record for this book is available from
the British Library.

Typeset by CenteaCet Limited, Cambridge
Printed and bound in Great Britain by
Mackays of Chatham PLC, Chatham, Kent

For Two Josephines

CONTENTS

Contents

Contents

FOREWORD

It's been my fate to read a great many books on how to be a writer, how to write, how to write fiction. Most are full of goodwill and bread-and-butter advice, and often have a fair degree of practical use: teaching a would-be author the basic rules of storytelling and genre, exploring the organizational problems and difficulties that arise in the writing of novels, short stories, poems and plays. As you'd guess, the best are usually those written by distinguished writers themselves, the people who have learned the hard way and produced the finest results. But on the whole it's an uninspired genre, and the biggest danger is that it teaches mechanical rules, simple practices, conventional routines – just those rules that are broken by any writer of originality. The essence of serious writing is that it's not a struggle to repeat what others have done, but a struggle not to. The most interesting writers do have a deep sense of the key rules and conventions of writing. But they're not trying to copy a genre, a tradition, a set of habits, but to extend them, through strength of vision, power of language, formal innovation. In other words, what makes good or great writing is not the simple ability to follow habits and customs; it's the presence of a strong and original vision that employs writing as a medium of exploration.

The crucial fact is that writing starts long before we begin writing this novel or that story – in the sensibility, self-control and originality of a particular writer. And the book that marks the great exception to the general rule that books with general rules are only of limited use is this one, Dorothea Brande's *Becoming a Writer*. First published in the USA in 1934, it has some limitations of its period: the writer Brande steers toward the typewriter is nowadays more likely to be using a word processor (that great aid to one of the chief literary tasks, revising and rewriting); the names of some of the writers she recommends could now be usefully replaced by others. But *Becoming a Writer* is a living classic among those who are interested in creative writing, for very good reason. This isn't a book about How to Write a Novel, nor how to write any particular kind of book at all. It's about what must happen before that: the mysterious process of first becoming a writer, acquiring the writerly instincts. It takes for granted that writing and the ability to do it begin long before pen is put to paper, the word processor switched on. It's born in temperament, desire, the management of one's instincts, impulses and feelings, the sensible organization of energy and effort. The book was written in Freudian times, and rightly assumes that writing is a psychological matter: at once a conscious activity and an unconscious one. Reconciling and balancing the two – making the unconscious conscious, and making the conscious tap the elements that are less than conscious – is an essential part not just of the process of writing, but becoming a writer in the first place.

Anyone who has taught that complicated enterprise called creative writing knows that, in the making of a writer, many different elements must always be kept in play. Good writers are generally, first and foremost, good readers; their instinct to explore what Brande calls the 'magic' of writing comes because they have been convinced by the power of what other writers have done. They're also a certain kind of reader, not simply satisfied to accept what others have achieved on their behalf, but interested in understanding, pursuing, developing how it's done. What pushes them onward is a strong sense of inner motivation, and an effective capacity to organize and manage the impulses, instincts and artistic techniques to which they're willing to devote their lives. One of the most truthful thoughts in this very truthful book is the repeated implication that only part of the business of writing can ever be consciously taught. Most has to be discovered, from within. What a teacher can do is usually something with the organization, the structure, the effective exploring and shaping, of impulses, ideas and imaginative energies that are already in play. Often these impulses are too general and undirected; they pursue no determined end, seek no particular reader, communicate no particular urgency. Sometimes the essential material is there, but the writer works in a rhetorical frenzy, not rooted in real feeling or honest observation, so that the writing offers us neither the clear vision nor a gift for truthful discovery.

Dorothea Brande's book is one other writers have found truthful because it touches on the real and familiar sensations of writing at the moment when it's practised, and because it emphasizes the essential doubleness of writing. Writing is will and imagination; it depends both on unbidden impulses and on careful, considered dedication to the tools of language, the techniques of composition, the powers of art. As she suggests, much writing comes out of a contradiction, between the conscious side, occupied by the craftsman and the critic, and the unconscious side, the 'artist's side.' As she says, it's possible to make them work in harmony, but the first step in the education is to 'teach yourself not as though you were one person, but two.' The value of the argument is that much writing is indeed born out of dream, fantasy, self-surprise; at the same time the writer is someone who acquires the capacity for organizing and constructing daily life in order to be capable of writing effectively, with a real sense of growth and development. The writer's problem is to turn the creative and critical skills of the imagination onto those elements the imagination has, within itself, already begun to create.

The other key point about the book is that it's written with the authority of the genuine teacher — someone who understands how important it is to bring out existing skills and creative instincts, and is capable of putting tasks and exercises in a significant and sensible order, so that one stage in a development or a self-analysis logically leads on to another. It rightly presumes that there is a process at work in becoming an artist, that it is difficult and owes much to the management of temperament, that although the instinctive and intuitional aspects of the self are important they are by no means everything. Brande suggests a series of specific exercises; the question is not so much whether they work as she says as how we can ourselves achieve what she's trying to produce — an aura of writing, a ready instinct for imaginative work, a willingness to open up to narrative impulse, a capacity to work consistently in the right state of mind, with the will and means to achieve. Writing is, to some extent at least, a writer's acquired habit; the rhythms of it, the particular styles we each possess in doing it, are practices we each teach ourselves in order to write continuously, and with a hope of doing ever better.

There are helpful golden rules: that one should always try to think as a writer, be a person on whom nothing is lost; that one should try, if possible, to work every day, or trust that on days when one's off, the process of composition still goes unconsciously on; that it is good to try to write even when there is ostensibly nothing to write about; that revision and self-criticism are a crucial facility; that nothing is finished until it has been through the careful sieve of your own objective judgement – for a writer must be an excellent self-reader. Brande's book gives various forms of practice intended to point the way to these things; but the crucial emphasis is on the distinctive originality each writer has to seek. Her chief point is a simple but fundamental one: the writing of a story, poem, or play is not simply the application of some proved and tested technique to a body of material already to hand. As she says: 'If a situation has caught your attention . . . it has meaning for you, and if you can find what that meaning is you have the basis for a story.' A writer 'discovers' a story; the story, using the writer's instinct and vision, then discovers itself. The distinctiveness of vision that she identifies, perhaps unfashionably, as 'genius' is a real and necessary element of serious creation. It's the spirit of oneself as one writes, the breathing of oneself into one's writing, the 'writer's magic' which is the goal of all the advice she has given.

The problem is indeed to 'become' a writer. Then, with a new kind of self-organization and self-under-standing, you can go on to apply to the best technical books you can find. I believe myself the most useful are the great, often very naked accounts of what major writers have done: Dostoevsky's notebooks, James' notebooks and prefaces, Virginia Woolf's diary, some of the literary interviews conducted in *The Paris Review* in recent years and published as *Writers at Work*. Brande's final 'prosaic pointers' belong to her day, but can easily be updated. Today we not only have word processors but pre-prepared software writing formats, and the means of, in effect, publishing ourselves. There are plenty of writers' handbooks to point the way on, to agents and publishers, editors and magazines, television companies and movie studios. The writers' situation in society is less lonely than it was in Brande's day, the experiences of writing far less remote, regularly chronicled in the media. But the hardest, the loneliest, the most uncertain time is at the beginning, when we are trying to become a writer. As a wise, sensible and honest guidebook to that – and the continued problems and possibilities of writing, once becoming has turned into being – Dorothea Brande's book simply can't be bettered.

Malcolm Bradbury

IN INTRODUCTION

For most of my adult life I have been engaged in the writing, the editing, or the criticizing of fiction. I took, and I still take, the writing of fiction seriously. The importance of novels and short stories in our society is great. Fiction supplies the only philosophy that many readers know; it establishes their ethical, social, and material standards; it confirms them in their prejudices or opens their minds to a wider world. The influence of any widely read book can hardly be overestimated. If it is sensational, shoddy, or vulgar our lives are the poorer for the cheap ideals which it sets in circulation; if, as so rarely happens, it is a thoroughly good book, honestly conceived and honestly executed, we are all indebted to it. The movies have not undermined the influence of fiction. On the contrary, they have extended its field, carrying the ideas which are already current among readers to those too young, too impatient, or too uneducated to read.

So I make no apology for writing seriously about the problems of fiction writers; but until two years ago I should have felt apologetic about adding another volume to the writer's working library. During the period of my own apprenticeship – and, I confess, long after that apprenticeship should have been over – I read every book on the technique of fiction, the constructing of plots, the handling of characters, that I could lay my hands on. I sat at the feet of teachers of various schools: I have heard the writing of fiction analyzed by a neo-Freudian; I submitted myself to an enthusiast who saw in the glandular theory of personality determination an inexhaustible mine for writers in search of characters; I underwent instruction from one who drew diagrams and from another who started with a synopsis and slowly inflated it into a completed story. I have lived in a literary 'colony' and talked to practicing writers who regarded their calling variously as a trade, a profession, and (rather sheepishly) as an art. In short, I have had firsthand experience with almost every current 'approach' to the problems of writing, and my bookshelves overflow with the works of other instructors whom I have not seen in the flesh.

But two years ago – after still more years spent in reading for publishers, choosing the fiction for a magazine of national circulation, writing articles, stories, reviews and more extended criticism, conferring informally with editors and with authors of all ages about their work – I began, myself, to teach a class in fiction writing. Nothing was further from my mind, on the evening of my first lecture, than adding to the top-heavy literature on the subject. Although I had been considerably disappointed in most of the books I had read and all the classes I had attended, it was not until I joined the ranks of instructors that I realized the true basis of my discontent.

That basis of discontent was that the difficulties of the average student or amateur writer begin long before he has come to the place where he can benefit by technical instruction in story writing. He himself is in no position to suspect that truth. If he were able to discover for himself the reasons for his aridity the chances are that he would never be found enrolled in any class at all. But he only vaguely knows that successful writers have overcome the difficulties which seem almost insuperable to him; he believes that accepted authors have some magic, or at the very lowest, some trade secret, which, if he is alert and attentive, he may surprise. He suspects, further, that the teacher who offers his services knows that magic, and may drop a word about it which will prove an Open Sesame to him. In the hope of hearing it, or surprising it, he will sit doggedly through a series of instructions in story types and plot forming and technical problems which have no relation to his own dilemma. He will buy or borrow every book with 'fiction' in the title; he will read any symposium by authors in which they tell their methods of work.

In almost every case he will be disappointed. In the opening lecture, within the first few pages of his book, within a sentence or two of his authors' symposium, he will be told rather shortly that 'genius cannot be taught'; and there goes his hope glimmering. For whether he knows it or not, he is in search of the very thing that is denied him in that dismissive sentence. He may never presume to call the obscure impulse to set down his picture of the world in words by the name of 'genius,' he may never dare to bracket himself for a moment with the immortals of writing, but the disclaimer that genius cannot be taught, which most teachers and authors seem to feel must be stated as early and as abruptly as possible, is the death knell of his real hope. He had longed to hear that there *was* some magic about writing, and to be initiated into the brotherhood of authors.

This book, I believe, will be unique; for I think he is right. I think there is such a magic, and that it is teachable. This book is all about the writer's magic.

– Chapter One –

THE FOUR DIFFICULTIES

So, having made my apologies, and stated my belief, I am going, from now on, to address myself solely to those who hope to write.

There is a sort of writer's magic. There is a procedure which many an author has come upon by happy accident or has worked out for himself which can, in part, be taught. To be ready to learn it you will have to go by a rather roundabout way, first considering the main difficulties which you will meet, then embarking on simple, but stringently self-enforced, exercises to overcome those difficulties. Last of all you must have the faith, or the curiosity, to take one odd piece of advice which will be unlike any of the exhortations that have come your way in classrooms or in textbooks.

In one other way, beside the admission that there is an initiate's knowledge in writing, I am going to depart from the usual procedure of those who offer handbooks for young authors. Open book after book devoted to the writer's problems: in nine cases out of ten you will find, well toward the front of the volume, some very gloomy paragraphs warning you that you may be no writer at all, that you probably lack taste, judgment, imagination, and every trace of the special abilities necessary to turn yourself from an aspirant into an artist, or even into a passable craftsman. You are likely to hear that your desire to write is perhaps only an infantile exhibitionism, or to be warned that because your friends think you a great writer (as if they ever did!) the world cannot be expected to share that fond opinion. And so on, most tiresomely. The reasons for this pessimism about young writers are dark to me. Books written for painters do not imply that the chances are that the reader can never be anything but a conceited dauber, nor do textbooks on engineering start out by warning the student that because he has been able to make a grasshopper out of two rubber bands and a matchstick he is not to think that he is likely ever to be an honor to his chosen profession.

Perhaps it is true that self-delusion most often takes the form of a belief that one can write; as to that I cannot say. My own experience has been that there is no field where one who is in earnest about learning to do good work can make such enormous strides in so short a time. So I am going to write this book for those who are fully in earnest, trusting to their good sense and their intelligence to see to it that they learn the elements of sentence and paragraph structure, that they already see that when they have chosen to write they have assumed an obligation toward their reader to write as well as they are able, that they will have taken (and are still taking) every opportunity to study the masters of English prose writing, and that they have set up an exigent standard for themselves which they work without intermission to attain.

It may be that it is only my extraordinary good fortune that I have met more writers of whom these things are true than deluded imbecile scribblers. But tragically enough I have met a number of sensitive young men and women who have very nearly been persuaded, because they had come up against one of the obstacles to writing which we are shortly going to consider, that they were unfit to write at all. Sometimes the desire to write overcame the humiliation they had had to undergo; but others dropped back into a life with no creative outlet, unhappy, thwarted, and restless. I hope this book persuades some who are hesitating on the verge of abandoning writing to make a different decision.

In my experience four difficulties have turned up again and again. I am consulted about them far oftener than I am asked for help in story structure or character delineation. I suspect that every teacher hears the same complaints, but that, being seldom a practicing author, he tends to dismiss them as out of his field, or to see in them evidence that the troubled student has not the true vocation. Yet it is the very pupils who are most obviously gifted who suffer from these disabilities, and the more sensitively organized they are the higher the hazard seems to them. Your embryo journalist or hack writer seldom asks for help of any sort; he is off after agents and editors while his more serious brother-in-arms is suffering the torments of the damned because of his insufficiencies. Yet instruction in writing is oftenest aimed at the oblivious tradesman of fiction, and the troubles of the artist are dismissed or overlooked.

The Difficulty of Writing at All

First there is the difficulty of writing *at all*. The full, abundant flow that must be established if the writer is to be heard from simply will not begin. The stupid conclusion that if he cannot write easily he has mistaken his career is sheer nonsense. There are a dozen reasons for the difficulty which should be canvassed before the teacher is entitled to say that he can see no signs of hope for this pupil.

It may be that the root of the trouble is youth and humility. Sometimes it is self-consciousness that stems the flow. Often it is the result of misapprehensions about writing, or it arises from an embarrassment of scruples: the beginner may be waiting for the divine fire of which he has heard to glow unmistakably, and may believe that it can only be lighted by a fortuitous spark from above. The particular point to be noted just here is that this difficulty is *anterior* to any problems about story structure or plot building, and that unless the writer can be helped past it there is very likely to be no need for technical instruction at all.

The 'One-Book Author'

Second, and far more often than the layman would believe, there is the writer who has had an early success but is unable to repeat it. Here again there is a cant explanation which is offered whenever this difficulty is met: this type of writer, we are assured, is a 'one-book author'; he has written a fragment of autobiography, has unburdened himself of his animus against his parents and his background, and, being relieved, cannot repeat his tour de force. But obviously he does not consider himself a one-book author, or we should hear nothing more from him. Moreover, all fiction is, in the sense used here, autobiographical, and yet there are fortunate authors who go on shaping, recombining, and objectifying the items of their experience into a long series of satisfactory books or stories. No; he is right in considering the sudden stoppage of his gift a morbid symptom, and right, usually, in thinking it can be relieved.

It is evident, if this writer had a deserved success, that he already knows something, presumably a great deal, of the technical end of his art. His trouble is not there, and, except by happy accident, no amount of counsel and advice about technique will break the deadlock. He is, in some ways, more fortunate than the beginner who cannot learn to write fluently, for at least he has given evidence of his ability to set down words in impressive order. But his first impatience at being unable to repeat his success can pass into discouragement and go on to actual despair, and an excellent author may be lost in consequence.

The Occasional Writer

The third difficulty is a sort of combination of the first two: there are writers who can, at wearisomely long intervals, write with great effectiveness. I have had a pupil whose output was one excellent short story each year – hardly enough to satisfy either body or spirit. The sterile periods were torture to her; the world, till she could write again, a desert waste. Each time she found herself unable to work she was certain she could never repeat her success, and, on first acquaintance, she very nearly persuaded me of it. But when the cycle was lived through from start to finish she always wrote again, and wrote well.

Here again no technical instruction can touch the difficulty. Those who suffer from these silences in which not one idea seems to arise, not one sentence to come irresistibly to the mind's surface, may write like artists and craftsmen when they have once broken the spell. The teacher-consultant must form a definite idea of the root of the trouble and give counsel accordingly. It may be, again, that some notion of waiting for the lightning of inspiration to strike is behind the matter. Often it is the result of such ideals of perfection as can hardly bear the light of day. Sometimes, but rarely, a kind of touchy vanity is at work, which will not risk any rebuff and so will not allow anything to be undertaken which is not assured in advance of acceptance.

The Uneven Writer

The fourth difficulty actually has a technical aspect: it is the inability to carry a story, vividly but imperfectly apprehended, to a successful conclusion. Writers who complain of this are often able to start a story well, but find it out of control after a few pages. Or they will write a good story so drily and sparely that all its virtues are lost. Occasionally they cannot motivate their central action adequately, and the story carries no conviction.

It is quite true that those who find themselves in this pass can be greatly helped by learning about structure, about the various forms which the story may take, of the innocuous 'tricks of the trade' which will help a story over the stile. But even here the real difficulty has set in long before the story *form* is in question. The author has not the self-confidence necessary to present his idea well, or he is too inexperienced to know how his characters would act in real life, or he is too shy to write as fully and emotionally as he needs to write if his story is to come to life. The writer who turns out one weak, embarrassed, or abruptly told story after another obviously needs something more than to have his individual manuscripts criticized for him. As soon as possible he must learn to trust his own feeling for the story, and to relax in the telling, until he has learned to use the sure, deft stroke of the man who is master of his medium. So even this dilemma comes down, after all, to being a trouble in the writer's personality rather than a defect in his technical equipment.

The Difficulties Not in Technical Equipment

Those are the four difficulties oftenest met at the outset of an author's writing life. Almost everyone who buys books on fiction writing, or takes classes in the art of the short story, suffers from one or another of these troubles, and until they have been overcome he is able to get very little benefit from the technical training which will be so valuable to him later. Occasionally writers are stimulated enough by the classroom atmosphere to turn out stories during the course; but they stop writing the moment that stimulus is withdrawn. An astonishing number who really want ardently to write are unable even to do assigned themes, yet they turn up hopefully – sometimes year after year. Obviously they are looking for help that is not being given them; and obviously they are in earnest – ready to spend what time, effort, and money they can to emerge from the class of novices and 'yearners' and take their place among productive artists.

Chapter Two

WHAT WRITERS ARE LIKE

If these are the difficulties, then we must try to cure them where they arise – in the life and attitudes and habits, in the very character itself. After you have begun to see what it is to be a writer, after you learn how the artist functions and also learn to act in the same way, after you have arranged your affairs and your relations so that they help you instead of hinder you on your way toward the goal you have chosen, those books on your shelves on the technique of fiction, or those others which set up models of prose style and story structure for emulation, will look quite different to you, and be infinitely more helpful. This volume is not intended to replace those books on craftsmanship. There are some handbooks so valuable that no writer should be without them. In the appended bibliography I give the titles of those I have found most helpful for myself and for my pupils; I have no doubt that the list could be doubled or trebled to advantage. This book is not even a companion volume to such works as those; it is a preliminary to them. If it is successful it will teach the beginner not how to write, but how to be a writer; and that is quite another thing.

Cultivating a Writer's Temperament

First of all, then, becoming a writer is mainly a matter of cultivating a writer's temperament. Now the very word 'temperament' is justly suspect among well-balanced persons, so I hasten to say that it is no part of the program to inculcate a wild-eyed bohemianism, or to set up moods and caprices as necessary accompaniments of the author's life. On the contrary; the moods and tempers, when they actually exist, are the symptoms of the artist's personality gone wrong – running off into waste effort and emotional exhaustion.

I say 'when they actually exist,' for much of the bumptious idiocy which the average man believes is an inalienable part of the artist's makeup has no being except in the eye of the beholder. He has heard tales of artists all his life, and very frequently he really believes 'poetic license' to mean that the artist claims the right to ignore every moral code which inconveniences him. What the non-writer thinks about the artist would be of little account if it did not influence those who would like to write; they are persuaded against their will and their better sense that there is something fearful and dangerous in an artist's life, and some of the very shyness which we have seen as a mischief-maker comes from their giving too much credence to such popular notions.

False and Real Artists

After all, very few of us are born into homes where we see true examples of the artistic temperament, and since artists do certainly conduct their lives – necessarily – on a different pattern from the average man of business, it is very easy to misunderstand what he does and why he does it when we see it from the outside. The picture of the artist as a monster made up of one part vain child, one part suffering martyr, and one part *boulevardier* is a legacy to us from the last century, and a remarkably embarrassing inheritance. There is an earlier and healthier idea of the artist than that, the idea of the genius as a man more versatile, more sympathetic, more studious than his fellows, more catholic in his tastes, less at the mercy of the ideas of the crowd.

The grain of truth in the fin de siècle notion, though, is this: the author of genius does keep till his last breath the spontaneity, the ready sensitiveness, of a child, the 'innocence of eye' that means so much to the painter, the ability to respond freshly and quickly to new scenes, and to old scenes as though they were new; to see traits and characteristics as though each were new-minted from the hand of God instead of sorting them quickly into dusty categories and pigeon-holing them without wonder or surprise; to feel situations so immediately and keenly that the word 'trite' has hardly any meaning for him; and always to see 'the correspondences between things' of which Aristotle spoke two thousand years ago. This freshness of response is vital to the author's talent.

The Two Sides of a Writer

But there is another element to his character, fully as important to his success. It is adult, discriminating, temperate, and just. It is the side of the artisan, the workman and the critic rather than the artist. it must work continually with and through the emotional and childlike side, or we have no work of art. If either element of the artist's character gets too far out of hand the result will be bad work, or no work at all. The writer's first task is to get these two elements of his nature into balance, to combine their aspects into one integrated character. And the first step toward that happy result is to split them apart for consideration and training!

'Dissociation' Not Always Psychopathic

We have all read a great many Sunday 'feature stories,' magazine articles, and books of popularized psychology; so our first impulse is to shy violently away from the words 'dissociation of personality.' A dual personality, to the reader who has a number of half-digested notions about the constitution of the mind, is an unlucky fellow who should be in a psychopathic ward; or, at the happiest, a flighty, hysterical creature. Nevertheless, every author is a very fortunate sort of dual personality, and it is this very fact that makes him such a bewildering, tantalizing, irritating figure to the plain man of affairs who flatters himself that he, at least, is all of a piece. But there is no scandal and no danger in recognizing that you have more than one side to your character. The journals and letters of men of genius are full of admissions of their sense of being dual or multiple in their nature: there is always the workaday man who walks, and the genius who flies. The idea of the alter ego, the other self, or higher self, recurs wherever genius becomes conscious of its own processes, and we have testimony for it in age after age.

Everyday Examples of Dual Personality

Indeed, the dual character of the genius is almost a commonplace. As a matter of fact, it is a commonplace for all of us, to some extent. Everyone has had the experience of acting with a decision and neatness in an emergency which seem later to him to savor of the miraculous; this was the figure which Frederick W. H. Myers used to convey his idea of the activity of genius. Or there is the experience of the 'second wind' that comes after long grinding effort, when suddenly fatigue seems to drop away and a new character to arise like a phoenix from the exhausted mind or body; and the work that went so haltingly begins to flow under the hand. There is the obscurer, but cognate, experience of having reached a decision, solved a problem, while we slept, and finding the decision good, the solution valid. All these everyday miracles bear a relation to genius. At such moments the conscious and the unconscious conspire together to bring about the maximum effect; they play into each other's hands, supporting, strengthening, and supplementing each other, so that the resulting action comes from the full, integral personality, bearing the authority of the undivided mind.

The man of genius is one who habitually (or very often, or very successfully) acts as his less gifted brothers only rarely do. He not only acts *in* an event, but he creates an event, leaving his record of the moment on paper, canvas, or in stone. As it were, he makes his own emergency and acts in it, and his willingness both to instigate and perform marks him off from his more inert, less courageous comrades.

Everyone who has seriously wanted to write has some hint of this. Often it is in the very moment of vision that the first difficulties arise. Embarkation on the career is easy enough; an inclination to reverie, a love of books, the early discovery that it is not too difficult to turn a phrase – to find any or all of these things in one's first adolescent consciousness is to believe that one has found the inevitable, and not too formidable, vocation.

The Slough of Despond

But then comes the dawning comprehension of all that a writer's life implies: not easy day-dreaming, but hard work at turning the dream into reality without sacrificing all its glamour, not the passive following of someone else's story, but the finding and finishing of a story of one's own; not writing a few pages which will be judged for style or correctness alone, but the prospect of turning out paragraph after paragraph and page after page which will be read for style, content, and effectiveness. Nor is this by any means all the beginning writer foresees. He worries to think of his immaturity, and wonders how he ever dared to think he had a word worth saying. He gets as stagestruck at the thought of his unseen readers as any sapling actor. He discovers that when he is able to plan a story step by step, the fluency he needs to write it has flown out the window; or that when he lets himself go on a loose rein, suddenly the story is out of hand. He fears that he has a tendency to make his stories all alike, or paralyzes himself with the notion that he will never, when this story is finished, find another that he likes as well. He will begin to follow current reputations and harry himself because he has not this writer's humor or that one's ingenuity. He will find a hundred reasons to doubt himself and not one for self-confidence. He will suspect that those who encouraged him are too lenient, or too far from the market to know the standards of successful fiction. Or he will read the work of a real genius in words, and the discrepancy between that gift and his own will seem a chasm to swallow his hopes. In such a state, lightened now and again by moments when he feels his own gift alive and surging, he may stay for months or years.

Every writer goes through this period of despair. Without doubt many promising writers, and most of those who were never meant to write, turn back at this point and find a lifework less exacting. Others are able to find the other bank of their slough of despond, sometimes by inspiration, sometimes by sheer doggedness. Still others turn to books or counselors. But often they are unable to tell the source of their baffled discomfort; they may even assign the reasons for their feeling of fright to the wrong causes, and think that they miss effectiveness because they 'cannot write dialogue,' or 'are no good at plots' or 'make all the characters too stiff.' When they have worked as intensively as possible to overcome the weakness, only to find that their difficulties continue, there comes another unofficial weeding-out. Some drop away from this group; still others persist, even though they have reached the stage of dumb discomfort where they no longer feel that they can diagnose their own cases.

No ordeal by discouragement which editors, teachers, and older writers can devise is going to kill off the survivor of this type. What he needs to realize first is that he tried to do too much at once, and next, that although he started going about his self-education step by step, he took the wrong steps. Most of the methods of training the conscious side of the writer – the craftsman and the critic in him – are actually hostile to the good of the unconscious, the artist's side; and the converse of this proposition is likewise true. *But it is possible to train both sides of the character to work in harmony, and the first step in that education is to consider that you must teach yourself not as though you were one person, but two.*

– Chapter Three –

THE ADVANTAGES OF DUPLICITY

To see why training oneself to be a writer is a double task, let us go rapidly over the process of story formation.

The Process of Story Formation

Like any other art, creative writing is a function of the whole man. The unconscious must flow freely and richly, bringing at demand all the treasures of memory, all the emotions, incidents, scenes, intimations of character and relationship which it has stored away in its depths; the conscious mind must control, combine, and discriminate between these materials without hampering the unconscious flow. The unconscious will provide the writer with 'types' of all kinds – typical characters, typical scenes, typical emotional responses; the conscious will have the task of deciding which of these are too personal, too purely idiosyncratic to be material for art, and which of them are universal enough to be useful. It may also be called upon to add intentionally those special traits which turn too universal a figure into an individual character, to undertake the humanizing of a type-form – a necessity if the fiction is to convey a sense of reality.

Each writer's unconscious will be found to have, if I may put it so, a type-story of its own: because of the individual's history, he will tend to see certain dilemmas as dramatic and overlook others entirely, as he will also have his own idea of the greatest possible happiness and personal good. Of course, it follows that each writer's stories will always bear a fundamental likeness to each other. This need not be seen as a threat of monotony, but the conscious mind must be enough aware of it to alter, recombine, introduce elements of surprise and freshness into each new story project.

Because of the tendency of the unconscious to see things in types, it is the unconscious, in the long run, which dictates the form of the story. (But this will be taken up more fully later. All that needs pointing out here is that if this is so a great deal of instruction on plot making is a waste of time. Certain ingenuities can be suggested, the popular story of any given period can be isolated and studied, and formulas for its writing can be devised; but unless a given formula is already congenial to the student he will get little help by attempting to model his own work upon it.) At any rate, the story arises in the unconscious. It then appears, sometimes only vaguely prefigured, at other times astonishingly definite, in the consciousness. There it is scrutinized, pruned, altered, strengthened, made more spectacular or less melodramatic; and is returned into the unconscious for the final synthesis of its elements. After a period of intense activity – which, however, goes on at so deep a level that the author himself occasionally feels he has 'forgotten' or 'lost' his idea – it once again signals to the conscious that the work of synthesis has been done; and the actual writing of the story begins.

The 'Born Writer'

In the genius, or the 'born writer,' we see this process taking place so smoothly and often so rapidly that even this overcompressed scheme seems to misrepresent the story's history. But the genius, you must remember, is the man who by some fortunate accident of temperament or education can put his unconscious completely at the service of his reasonable intention, whether or not he is aware that this is so. The proof of this statement will emerge later, for the process of making a writer is the process of teaching the novice to do by artifice what the born writer does spontaneously.

Unconscious and Conscious

The unconscious is shy, elusive, and unwieldy, but it is possible to learn to tap it at will, and even to direct it.

The conscious mind is meddlesome, opinionated, and arrogant, but it can be made subservient to the inborn talent through training. By isolating as far as possible the functions of these two sides of the mind, even by considering them not merely as aspects of the same mind but as separate personalities, we can arrive at a kind of working metaphor, impossible to confuse with reality, but infinitely helpful in self-education.

The Two Persons of the Writer

So, for a period, while the conception is useful to you, think of yourself as two-persons-in-one. There will be a prosaic, everyday, practical person to bear the brunt of the day's encounters. It will have plenty of virtues to offset its stolidity; it must learn to be intelligently critical, detached, tolerant, while at the same time remembering that its first function is to provide suitable conditions for the artist-self. The other half of your dual nature may then be as sensitive, enthusiastic, and partisan as you like; only it will not drag those traits out into the workaday world. It distinctly will not be allowed, by the cherishing elderly side, to run the risk of being made miserable by trying to cope emotionally with situations which call only for reason, or of looking ludicrous to the unindulgent observer.

The Transparent Barrier

The first advantage that will be gained by your innocent duplicity is that you will have erected a transparent barrier between you and the world, behind which you can grow into your artistic maturity at your own pace. The average person writes just too much and not quite enough to have any great opinion of an author's life. It is unfortunate, but the unimaginative citizen finds something exquisitely funny about the idea that one aspires to make a name and a living by any such process as 'stringing words together.' He finds it presumptuous when an acquaintance announces that he has elected to give the world his opinion in writing, and punishes the presumption by merciless teasing. If you feel called upon to correct this unimaginative attitude you will have opportunities enough to keep you busy for a lifetime, but you will not – unless you have an extraordinary amount of energy – have much strength left for writing. The same plain man reacts as impulsively and naively to the successful writer. He is awestruck in his presence, but he is also very uncomfortable. Nothing but witchcraft, he seems to believe, could have made another human being so wise in the ways of his kind. He will turn self-conscious, and act either untypically or refuse to act at all; and if you alarm him you will find yourself barred from one source of your material. This is a low piece of advice to give, but I give it without apology: keep still about your intentions, or you will startle your quarry.

Keep Your Own Counsel

Then, too, the writer is at a disadvantage shared by no novice of the other arts. He does use the medium of ordinary conversation, of friendly letters and business letters, when he exercises his profession; and he has no impressive paraphernalia to impose respect on the layman. Now that everyone has his portable typewriter, not even that badge of his profession is left to the young writer. A musical instrument, canvas, clay, carry their own persuasiveness by seeming exotic to the uninitiated. Even a good singing voice does not issue from every throat. Until your name has been in print again and again you may get only teasing for your pains if you prematurely announce your allegiance to writing. At that, most young writers would benefit by taking a leaf from the practitioners of other arts; the violinist does not carry around his violin, the artist does not carry his palette and brushes, unless he is intending to use them, either privately or before a well-disposed audience. Give yourself the advantage of the same discretion, at least while you are finding your feet.

One excellent psychological reason for an author to keep his profession to himself is that if you confess so much you are likely to go further and talk of the things you mean to write. Now words are your medium, and effective use of them your profession; but your unconscious self (which is your wishful part) will not care whether the words you use are written down or talked to the world at large. If you are for the moment fortunate enough to have a responsive audience you often suffer for it later. You will have created your story and reaped your reward in approval or shocked disapproval; in either case you will have hit your mark. Afterward you will find yourself disinclined to go on with the laborious process of writing that story at full length; unconsciously you will consider it as already done, a twice-told tale. If you can conquer the disinclination to write you may still find that a slightly flat, uninterested note creeps in, in spite of you. So practice a wise taciturnity. When you have completed a fair first draft you can, if you like, offer it for criticism and advice; but to talk too early is a grave mistake.

There are other advantages in considering yourself a two-in-one character. It should not be your sensitive, temperamental self which bears the burden of your relations with the outside world of editors, teachers, or friends. Send your practical self out into the world to receive suggestions, criticisms, or rejections; by all means see to it that it is your prosaic self which reads rejection slips! Criticism and rejection are not personal insults, but your artistic component will not know that. It will quiver and wince and run to cover, and you will have trouble in luring it out again to observe and weave tales and find words for all the thousand shades of feeling that go to make up a story.

Your 'Best Friend and Severest Critic'

For another thing, your writing self is an instinctive, emotional creature, and if you are not careful you will find yourself living the life that will give you the least annoyance and the greatest ease instead of a life that will continually feed and stimulate your talent. The 'artistic temperament' is usually perfectly satisfied to exercise itself in reverie and amuse itself in solitude, and only once in a long while will the impulse to write rise spontaneously to the surface. If you leave it to the more sensitive side of your nature to set the conditions of work and living for you, you may find yourself at the end of your days with very little to show for the gift you were born with. A far better idea is to realize from the start that you are subject to certain caprices of action, and to study yourself objectively until you find which of your impulses are sound and which are likely to lead you into the bogs of inertia and silence. At first you will find it a great bore to be forever examining yourself for tendencies and habits; later you will find it second nature. Still later you will come to enjoy it rather too much, and the same critical attention will have to be given to the task of turning your scrutiny *away* from your own processes when your analysis has passed the stage where it bears beneficial fruits. In short, you will have to learn to be your own best friend and severest critic – mature, indulgent, stern and yielding by turns.

The Right Recreation

Observe, though, that you are to be your own best friend – not simply your stern and disciplinary elder. No one else will be in a position to discover for you what is best in the way of stimulation, amusement, and friends. Perhaps music (however little you know about music) may have the effect of starting up the obscure internal processes which send you to the typewriter. In that case it will be the task of your elder self to find and purvey music to you – and to see that you are not put on the defensive when you are questioned about your astonishing taste for symphony orchestras or Negro spirituals. You will find, too, that some friends are excellent for you as a writer who are worthless to you otherwise – and vice versa. Too stimulating a social life can be as hard on a budding talent as none at all. Only observation will show you the effect of any group or person *on you as a writer*. Seeing a dull soul whom you doggedly adore, or a brilliant friend who irritates you, may have to be treated as a very special form of indulgence, to be yielded to only rarely. If you feel, after an evening with the stolid friend, that the world is a dry and dusty place, or if you are exasperated to the point of speechlessness by your brilliant acquaintance, not the warmest emotion for them will justify your seeing much of them while you are trying to learn to write. You will have to find other acquaintances, persons who, for some mysterious reason, leave you full of energy, feed you with ideas, or, more obscurely still, have the effect of filling you with self-confidence and eagerness to write.

Friends and Books

If you are not fortunate enough to find them – well, you will discover fairish substitutes on library shelves, and occasionally in the strangest guises. I had a pupil who battened on medical case reports, and another who recorded that a few hours with a popular scientific monthly, which she could hardly understand in spite of its being insultingly elementary, induced in her such a feeling of being glutted with neat, hard little facts that she ran off to retrieve the balance by a debauch of imaginative writing. I know a popular author who abhors the works of John Galsworthy, but something in Galsworthy's rhythm starts up his own desire to write; he alleges that after a few pages of *The Forsyte Saga* he can hear an 'internal hum' which soon turns into sentences and paragraphs; on the other hand, Wodehouse, whom he considers a past master of modern humorous writing, plunges him into such depths of despond about his own performance that he takes care not to read the latest Wodehouse book until he has finished whatever he has in hand. Watch for a while, and see which authors are your meat and which your poison.

When the actual writing is to be done, your elder

self must stand aside, only murmuring a suggestion now and again on such matters as your tendency to use repetitions, or to suggest that you are being too verbose, or that the dialogue is getting out of hand. Later you will call on it to consider the completed draft, or section, and with its help you will alter the manuscript to get the best possible effects. But at the time of writing, nothing is more confusing than to have the alert, critical, overscrupulous rational faculty at the forefront of your mind. The tormenting doubts of one's own ability, the self-conscious muteness that drops like a pall over the best story ideas, come from consulting the judge in oneself at the moment when it is the storyteller's turn to be in the ascendant. It is not easy at first to inhibit the running verdicts on every sentence, almost every word, that is written, but once the flow of the story has well set in, the critical faculty will be content to wait its turn.

The Arrogant Intellect

There is no arrogance like that of the intellect, and one of the dangers, as we have said, of studying the technique of story writing too solemnly is that the reason is confirmed in its delusion of being the more important member of the writing team. It is not. Its duties are indispensable but secondary; they come before and after the period of intensive writing. You will find that if you cannot rein in your intellect during this period it will be forever offering pseudo-solutions to you, tampering with motives, making the characters 'literary' (which is often to make them stereotyped and unnatural), or protesting that the story which seemed so promising when it first dawned in your consciousness is really trite or implausible.

The Two Selves Not at War

But now I am in danger of making it seem that these two halves of the writing personality are at war with each other, when it is the exact contrary that is true. When each has found its place, when each is performing the functions which are proper to it, they play endlessly back and forth into each other's hands, strengthening, inciting, relieving each other in such a way that the resulting personality, the integral character, is made more balanced, mellow, energetic, and profound. It is precisely when they are at war that we get the unhappy artist – the artist who is working against the grain, or against his sober judgment, or, saddest of all, is unable to work. The most enviable writers are those who, quite often unanalytically and unconsciously, have realized that there are different facets to their nature and are able to live and work with now one, now another, in the ascendant.

The First Exercise

Now we come to the first exercise of a book which will be full of exercises. Its purpose is to show you how simple it is to see oneself objectively.

You are near a door. When you come to the end of this chapter put the book aside, get up, and go through that door. From the moment you stand on the threshold *turn yourself into your own object of attention.* What do you look like, standing there? How do you walk? What, if you knew nothing about yourself, could be gathered of you, your character, your background, your purpose just there at just that minute? If there are people in the room whom you must greet, how do you greet them? How do your attitudes to them vary? Do you give any overt sign that you are fonder of one, or more aware of one, than of the rest?

There is no deep, dark, esoteric purpose behind this exercise. It is a primer lesson in considering oneself objectively, and should be dismissed from your mind when you have learned what you can from it. Another time try sitting at ease and – using no gestures at all – tell yourself step by step how you comb your hair. (You will find it harder than you think.) Again, follow yourself at any small routine task. A little later, take an episode of the day before; see yourself going up to it and coming away from it; and the episode itself as it might have looked to a stranger. At still another time think how you might have looked if you could follow yourself all day long from a little height. *Use the fiction maker's eye on yourself* to see how you would have appeared when you went in and out of houses, up streets and into stores, and back home at the end of the day.

Chapter Four

INTERLUDE:
ON TAKING ADVICE

With the best of intentions, we usually go about the formation of a new habit or the eradication of an old one in the manner most calculated to defeat our purpose. Whenever you come across a piece of advice in these pages I exhort you not to straighten your spine, grit your teeth, clench your fists, and go at the experiments with the light of do-or-die on your countenance.

Save Your Energy

We customarily expend enough energy in carrying out any simple action to bring about a result three times greater than the one we have in view. This is true from the simplest matters to the most complex and of physical effort as well as mental. If we climb stairs, we climb them with every muscle and organ laboring as though our soul's salvation were to be found on the top step, and the result is that we grow resentful at the dispro-portionate returns we receive from our expended energy. Or, putting a great deal more energy out than we can use, we must take it up, somehow, in purpose-less motion. Everyone has had the experience of push-ing a door that looked closed with more vigor than was necessary and of falling into the next room as a consequence. Or we have picked up some light object which looked deceptively heavy. If you notice your-self on such an occasion, you will see that you must make a slight backward motion merely to retrieve your balance.

Imagination Versus Will in Changing Habits

In mental effort we are likely to go still more widely astray from some childish notion that it is laudable to exert that 'slow, dead heave of the will' as often as possible. But in changing habits, you will find yourself getting your results far more quickly and with less 'backwash' if you engage your imagination in the process instead of calling out the biggest gun of your character equipment first.

This is not a plea to abandon the will. There will be times and occasions when only the whole weight of the will brought to bear on the matter in hand will prove effective. But the imagination plays a far greater role in our lives than we customarily acknowledge, although any teacher can tell you how great an advocate the imagination is when a child is to be led into a changed course.

Displacing Old Habits

Old habits are strong and jealous. They will not be displaced easily if they get any warning that such plans are afoot; they will fight for their existence with subtlety and persuasiveness. If they are too radically attacked they will revenge themselves; you will find, after a day or two of extraordinarily virtuous effort, all sorts of reasons why the new method is not good for you, why you should alter it in line with this or that old habit, or actually abandon it entirely. In the end you will have had no good from the new advice; but you will almost certainly feel that you have given it a fair trial and that it has failed. Your mistake will have been that you tired yourself out and exhausted your good intentions before you had a chance to see whether or not the program was the right one for you.

This is a very simple but rather spectacular experiment which you can make that will teach you more about your own processes of putting an idea into operation than pages of exhortation and explanation. It is this:

A Demonstration

Draw a circle on a sheet of paper, using the bottom of a tumbler or something of that circumference as the guide; then make a cross through it. Tie a heavy ring or a key on a string about four inches long. Hold the end of the string with the ring hanging like the weight of a pendulum over the intersection of the cross, about an inch above the paper. Now *think* around the circle, following the circumference with your eyes and ignoring the ring and cord entirely.

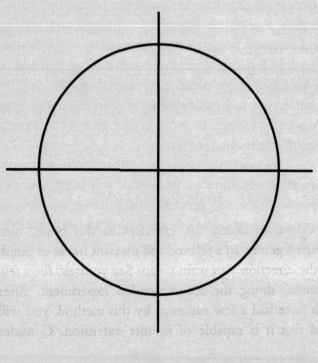

After a few moments the little pendulum will begin to swing around in the direction you have chosen, at first making a very small circle, but steadily widening out as it goes on. Then reverse the direction *in thought only* and follow the circle with your eyes in the other direction ... Now think up and down the perpendicular line; when that succeeds, shift to the horizontal. In each case the ring will stop for a moment and then begin to move in the direction of your thinking.

If you have not tried this experiment before you may feel that there is something uncanny about the result. There isn't. It is simply the neatest and easiest way of showing how important imagination can be in the sphere of action. Minute involuntary muscles take up the task for you. The will, you see, was hardly involved in the matter at all. And this, some French psychologists say, is the way to observe, in miniature, a 'faith cure' in operation. At the least, it should demonstrate that it is not necessary to brace every nerve and muscle to bring about a change in your daily life.

The Right Frame of Mind

So, then, in doing the exercises in this book, turn yourself gently, in a relaxed and pleasant frame of mind, in the direction you want to go. See yourself, for a few minutes, doing the recommended experiment. After you have had a few successes by this method, you will find that it is capable of infinite extension. Consider that all the minor inconveniences and interruptions of habits are to the end of making a full and effective life for yourself. Forget or ignore for a while all the difficulties you have let yourself dwell upon too often; refuse to consider, in your period of training, the possibility of failure. You are not at this stage of your career in any position to estimate your chances justly. Things which look difficult or impossible to you now will be seen in truer perspective when you have gone a little further. Later you can take an inventory of yourself from time to time, see what is easy for you and what you do badly or imperfectly. You can consider then what steps to take to correct these definite faults, and by that time you will be able to work on yourself profitably, without discouragement or bravado.

– Chapter Five –

HARNESSING THE UNCONSCIOUS

To begin with, you must teach the unconscious to flow into the channel of writing. Psychologists will forgive us for speaking so airily about 'teaching' the unconscious to do this or that. To all intents and purposes that is what happens; but less elegantly and more exactly we might say that the first step toward being a writer is to hitch your unconscious mind to your writing arm.

Wordless Daydreams

Most persons who are attracted by the idea of fiction at all are, or were in childhood, great dreamers. At almost any moment they can catch themselves, at some level, deep in reverie. Occasionally this reverie takes the form of recasting one's life, day by day or moment by moment, into a form somewhat nearer to the heart's desire: reconstructing conversations and arguments so that we come out with colors flying and epigrams falling around us like sparks, or imagining ourselves back in a simpler and happier period. Or adventure is coming toward us around the next corner, and we have already made up our minds as to the form it will take. All those naive and satisfying dreams of which we are the un-ashamed heroes or heroines are the very stuff of fiction, almost the *materia prima* of fiction. A little sophistication, a little experience, and we realize that we are not going to be allowed to carry off the honors in real life without a struggle; there are too many contenders for the role of leading lady or leading man. So, learning discretion and guile, we cast the matter a little differently; we objectify the ideal self that has caused us so much pleasure and write about him in the third person. And hundreds of our fellows, engaged secretly in just such daydreaming as our own, see themselves in our fictional characters and fall to reading when fatigue or disen-chantment robs them of their ability to see themselves under any glamorous guise. (Not, thank heaven, that this is the only reason a book is ever read; but undoubtedly it is the commonest one.)

The little Brontës, with their kingdom of Gonda-land, the infant Alcotts, young Robert Browning, and H. G. Wells all led an intensive dream-life which carried over into their maturity and took another form; and there are hundreds of authors who could tell the same stories of their youth. But there are probably thousands more who never grow up as writers. They are too self-conscious, too humble, or too solidly set in the habit of dreaming idly. After all, we begin our storytelling, usually, long before we are able to print simple words with infinite labor. It is little wonder that the glib unconscious should balk at the drudgery of committing its stories to writing.

Toward Effortless Writing

Writing calls on unused muscles and involves solitude and immobility. There is not much to be said for the recommendation, so often heard, to serve an apprenticeship to journalism if you intend to write fiction. But a journalist's career does teach two lessons which every writer needs to learn – that it is possible to write for long periods without fatigue, and that if one pushes on past the first weariness one finds a reservoir of unsuspected energy – one reaches the famous 'second wind.'

The typewriter has made the author's way more rocky than it was in the old days of quill and pen. However convenient the machine may be, there is no doubt about the muscular strain involved in typewriting; let any author tell you of rising stiff and aching from a long session. Moreover, there is the distraction set up by the little clatter of keys, and there is the strain of seeing the shafts continually dancing against the platen. But it is possible to make either typing or writing by hand second nature, so that muscular strain will not slow you down or keep you from writing.

So if you are to have the full benefit of the richness

of the unconscious you must learn to write easily and smoothly when the unconscious is in the ascendant.

The best way to do this is to rise half an hour, or a full hour, earlier than you customarily rise. Just as soon as you can – and without talking, without reading the morning's paper, without picking up the book you laid aside the night before – begin to write. Write anything that comes into your head: last night's dream, if you are able to remember it; the activities of the day before; a conversation, real or imaginary; an examination of conscience. Write any sort of early morning reverie, rapidly and uncritically. The excellence or ultimate worth of what you write is of no importance yet. As a matter of fact, you will find more value in this material than you expect, but your primary purpose now is not to bring forth deathless words, but to write any words at all which are not pure nonsense.

To reiterate, what you are actually doing is training yourself, in the twilight zone between sleep and the full waking state, simply *to write*. It makes no difference to the success of this practice if your paragraphs are amorphous, the thought vague or extravagant, the ideas hazy. Forget that you have any critical faculty at all; realize that no one need ever see what you are writing unless you choose to show it. You may, if you can, write in a notebook, sitting up in bed. If you can teach yourself to use the typewriter in this period, so much the better. Write as long as you have free time, or until you feel that you have utterly written yourself out.

The next morning begin without rereading what you have already done. Remember: you are to write *before* you have read at all. The purpose of this injunction will become clear later. Now all you need to concern yourself with is the mere performance of the exercise.

Double Your 'Output'

After a day or two you will find that there is a certain number of words that you can write easily and without strain. When you have found that limit, begin to push it ahead by a few sentences, then by a paragraph or two. A little later try to double it before you stop the morning's work.

Within a very short time you will find that the exercise has begun to bear fruit. The actual labor of writing no longer seems arduous or dull. You will have begun to feel that you can get as much (far more really) from a written reverie as from one that goes on almost wordlessly in the back of your mind. When you can wake, reach out for your pencil, and begin to write almost on one impulse, you will be ready for the next step. Keep the material you have written – under lock and key if that is the only way to save yourself from self-consciousness. It will have uses you can hardly foresee.

As you take up the next exercise, you can return, in this morning task, to the limit that seems easy and natural. (But you should be able to write more words than when you began.) Watch yourself carefully; if at any time you find you have slipped back into inactive reverie, it is time to exert pressure on yourself. Throughout your writing life, whenever you are in danger of the spiritual drought that comes to the most facile writer from time to time, put the pencil and paper back on your bedside table, and wake to write in the morning.

Chapter Six

WRITING ON SCHEDULE

At once, when you have put the suggestion in the last chapter into operation, you will find that you are more truly a *writer* than you ever were before. You will discover that now you have a tendency to cast the day's experiences into words, to foresee the use that you will make of an anecdote or episode that has come your way, to transform the rough material of life into fictional shape, more consistently than you did when writing was a sporadic, capricious occupation which broke out from time to time unaccountably, or was undertaken only when you felt that you had a story firmly within your grasp.

The moment you reach that stage, you are ready for the next step, which is to teach yourself to write at a given moment. The best way to do it is this:

Engaging to Write

After you have dressed, sit down for a moment by yourself and go over the day before you. Usually you can tell accurately enough what its demands and opportunities will be; roughly, at least, you can sketch out for yourself enough of your program to know when you will have a few moments to yourself. It need not be a very long time; fifteen minutes will do nicely, and there is almost no wage slave so driven that he cannot snatch a quarter of an hour from a busy day if he is in earnest about it. Decide for yourself when you will take that time for writing; for you are going to write in it. If your work falls off, let us say, after three-thirty in the afternoon, the fifteen minutes from four o'clock until quarter past four can safely be drafted as time of your own.

Well, then, at four o'clock you are going to write, come what may, and you are going to continue until the quarter-hour sounds. When you have made up your mind to that you are free to do whatever you like to do or must do.

A Debt of Honor

Now this is very important, and can hardly be emphasized too strongly: *you have decided to write at four o'clock, and at four o'clock write you must! No excuses can be given.* If at four o'clock you find yourself deep in conversation, you must excuse yourself and keep your engagement. Your agreement is a debt of honor, and must be scrupulously discharged; you have given yourself your word and there is no retracting it. If you must climb out over the heads of your friends at that hour, then be ruthless; another time you will find that you have taken some pains not to be caught in a dilemma of the sort. If to get the solitude that is necessary you must go into a washroom, go there, lean against the wall, and write. Write as you write in the morning – anything at all. Write sense or nonsense, limericks or blank verse; write what you think of your employer or your secretary or your teacher; write a story synopsis or a fragment of dialogue, or the description of someone you have recently noticed. However halting or perfunctory the writing is, *write*. If you must, you can write, 'I am finding this exercise remarkably difficult,' and say what you think are the reasons for the difficulty. Vary the complaint from day to day till it no longer represents the true state of affairs.

Extending the Exercise

For you are going to do this from day to day, but each time you are to choose a different hour. Try eleven o'clock, or a moment or two before or after lunch. Another time, promise yourself to write for fifteen minutes before you start for home in the evening; or fifteen minutes before you dine. The important thing is that *at* the moment, *on the dot of the moment*, you are to be writing, and that you teach yourself that no excuse of any nature can be offered when the moment comes.

While you are merely reading this recommendation you may be quite unable to see why it is put so emphatically. As you begin to put it into practice you will understand. There is a deep inner resistance to writing which is more likely to emerge at this point than in the earlier exercise. This will begin to 'look like business' to the unconscious, and the unconscious does not like these rules and regulations until it is well broken in to them; it is incorrigibly lazy in its busy-ness and given to finding the easiest way of satisfying itself. It prefers to choose its own occasions and to emerge as it likes. You will find the most remarkable series of obstacles presented to you under the similitude of common sense: Surely it will be just as satisfactory to write from 4:05 to 4:20? If you break out of a circle you are likely to be cross-questioned, so why not wait till the circle breaks up by itself and then take your fifteen minutes? In the morning you could hardly foresee that you were going to work yourself into a headache that day; can work done under the handicap of a headache possibly be fit to do? And so on and on. But you must learn to disregard every loophole the wily unconscious points out to you. If you consistently, doggedly, refuse to be beguiled, you will have your reward. The unconscious will suddenly give in charmingly, and begin to write gracefully and well.

Succeed, or Stop Writing

Right here I should like to sound the solemnest word of warning that you will find in this book: *If you fail repeatedly at this exercise, give up writing. Your resistance is actually greater than your desire to write, and you may as well find some other outlet for your energy early as late.*

These two strange and arbitrary performances – early morning writing, and writing by prearrangement – should be kept up till you write fluently at will.

Chapter Seven

THE FIRST SURVEY

When you have succeeded in establishing these two habits – early morning writing and writing by agreement with yourself – you have come a long way on the writer's path. You have gained, on the one hand, fluency, and on the other control, even though in an elementary way. You know a great deal more about yourself, in all likelihood, than you did when you embarked on the exercises. For one thing, you know whether it was easier to teach yourself to write on and on, or whether writing by prearrangement seemed more natural. Perhaps for the first time you see that if you want to write you can write, and that no life is actually so busy as to offer no opportunities if you are alert to find them. Then, too, you should begin to think it less than miraculous that writers can bring out book after book, having found in yourself the same inexhaustible resources that issue in the work of others. The physical mechanism of writing should have ceased to be tiring and begun to take its place as a simple activity. Your realization of the writer's life is probably more vivid, and nearer to the truth, than it was before – which is in itself a long stride to have taken.

Now it is time to consider yourself and your problems objectively again; and if you have followed the exercises well you should have plenty of material for an illuminating first survey.

Reading Your Work Critically

Up to this point it is best to resist the temptation to reread your productions. While you are training yourself into facility in writing and teaching yourself to start writing whenever and wherever opportunity offers, the less you turn a critical eye upon your own material the better – even for a cursory survey. The excellence or triteness of your writing was not the matter under consideration. But now, turning back to see what it may reveal under a dispassionate survey, you may find those outpourings very enlightening.

The Pitfalls of Imitation

You will remember that one of the conditions set was that you should not have read one word before beginning the morning's task, nor, if at all possible, so much as spoken until you have finished. This is the reason. We all live so surrounded by words that it is difficult for us to discover, without long experience, what our own rhythms are, and what subjects do really appeal to us. Those who are sensitive enough to want ardently to become writers are usually a little too suggestible for their own good. Consciously or not, they may have fallen into the temptation of imitating an established author. It may be a genuine master of writing; it may be (and too often is) the author whose work is having the greatest vogue at the moment. No one who has not taught fiction writing can believe how often a pupil will say some such thing as, 'Oh, I've just thought of the most marvelous Faulkner story!' or, more ambitiously, 'I think I can make a regular Virginia Woolf out of it.' The teacher who crassly says she would rather see a good story of the pupil's own is damned for a prig, or outspokenly argued with; for the notion that playing the sedulous ape to the extent of copying not only the prose style but the very philosophies and narrative forms of current popular authors seems to have been so inculcated in our apprentice writers that they genuinely believe they will become original authors by the process of imitation. The men and women who have served as their models, since they are writing from a strong native talent and according to their own personal tastes, grow, alter, change their styles and their 'formulas,' and the poor sedulous apes are left imitating the work of an outmoded period.

Discovering Your Strength

The best way to escape the temptation to imitate is to discover as early as possible one's own tastes and excellences. Here, in the sheaf of pages you have written during this period of habit-making, is priceless laboratory material for you. What, on the whole, *do* you write, when you set down the first things that occur to you? Try to read, now, as though you had the work of a stranger in your hands, and to discover there what the tastes and talents of this alien writer may be. Put aside every preconception about your work. Try to forget any ambitions or hopes or fears you may have entertained, and see what you would decide was the best field for this stranger if he were to consult you. The repetitions, the recurrent ideas, the frequent prose forms in these pages will give you your clues. They will show you where your *native* gift lies, whether or not you eventually decide to specialize in it. There is no reason to believe that you can write only one type of work, that you may not be fully as successful in some other line; but this examination will show you where your richest and most easily tapped vein lies.

In my experience, the pupil who sets down the night's dream, or recasts the day before into ideal form, who takes the morning hour to write a complete anecdote or a passage of sharp dialogue, is likely to be the short story writer in embryo. Certain types of character sketching, when it is brief and concerned with rather general (or even obvious) traits, point the same way. A subtler analysis of characters, a consideration of motives, acute self-examination (as distinct from romanticizing one's actions), the contrasting of different characters faced by the same dilemma, most often indicate the novelist. A kind of musing introspection or of speculation only sketched in is found in the essay writer's notebook, although with a grain of drama added, and with the particularizing of an abstract speculation by assigning the various elements of the problem to characters who act out the idea, there is promise of the more meditative type of novelist.

When this stage of instruction is reached there is often in my classes a burst of highly stimulating activity. Seeing the possibilities in the writing which they now feel came almost without effort, the pupils frequently branch into some type of work which they look on simply as recreation, and hammer away on their more difficult problems in their 'working' time. These spontaneous manuscripts are usually very interesting, and often, with some shaping, can be turned into satisfactory finished work. They are a little rambling, a little discursive, but they have a fresh, unforced tone which is striking. About this time you will find that your work is already less patchy and uneven; you are striking your own stride and finding your own rhythm, as well as discovering which subjects have a perennial interest for you.

A Footnote for Teachers

Here I should like to add a footnote for other teachers, rather than for students of writing. I think that holding up the work of each pupil in class for the criticism of the others is a thoroughly pernicious practice, and it does not become harmless simply by allowing the manuscript to be read without assigning its authorship publicly. The ordeal is too trying to be taken with equanimity, and a sensitive writer can be thrown out of his stride deplorably by it, whether or not the criticism is favorable. It is seldom that the criticism *is favorable*, when a beginner is judged by the jury of his peers. They seem to need to demonstrate that, although they are not yet writing quite perfectly themselves, they are able to see all the flaws in a story which is read to them, and they fall upon it tooth and fang. Until self-confidence arises naturally, and the pupil asks for group criticism, his work should be treated as utterly confidential by the teacher. Each will have his own rate of growth and it can only go on steadily if not endangered by the setbacks that come from embarrassment and self-consciousness. I recommend an almost inhuman taciturnity to my students, at least about work that is being done at the moment. There have been weeks when I have had nothing at all from the best workers in the class, only to have three or four full-length manuscripts from a single pupil at the end of the silent period. Beyond stipulating that each pupil must follow the exercises as they are given out, whether or not I see the material which is written from day to day, I assign no tasks.

– Chapter Eight –

THE CRITIC AT WORK
ON HIMSELF

Now, we will suppose, you have a kind of rough preliminary idea of yourself as a writer. It will be a very rough idea, still distorted by humility in some directions and overconfidence in others, but at least it will bear enough resemblance to your ultimate professional self to be worth working on. Even in this unfinished state you will realize that there are definite things which you can do for yourself that will improve the quality of your writing, provide you with occasions for writing, or stimulate you so that writing will follow naturally. It is time now to call on your prosaic side for the services it can render you. (As a matter of fact, it will already have been called on to read the material and find your self-revealed tastes, but that was only preliminary.) There are a hundred things it can do for you as soon as you have given it this much material to work on. If it is called in too soon, though, it hampers you more than it helps.

Here you are then, with all these pages and notebooks to be examined by your common sense, everyday character. By the cursory examination recommended in the last chapter you have already found the more obvious trends in your own work. Now it is time to be more specific, and to examine in detail what you have done. Your workaday self has been standing aside while you were about the business of teaching your unconscious to flow whenever you could find a moment for it; you will find now that it has been closely following the process, remarking your successes and failures, and getting ready with suggestions.

A Critical Dialogue

The next few paragraphs are much more naive and more outrageously dual than any dialogue you will ever have with yourself, but some such interchange as this between the sides of your nature should now take place:

'Do you know, I find that you write dialogue very well; you evidently have a good ear. But your passages of description aren't well done. They're stilted.'

Here the culprit will probably murmur something about liking to write dialogue, but feeling silly when describing anything without the protection of quotation marks.

'Of course you love to write dialogue,' you must return, 'just *because* you do it well. But don't you realize that if you can't do straight passages and transitions smoothly you're going to get a jerky story? You'd better make up your mind, I should say, whether you want to write fiction or to specialize in playwriting. Either way, you've got a lot of work to do.'

'Which should *you* say? That's almost as much in your department as mine?'

'Well, fiction, on the whole. You don't show much interest yet in dramatic and spectacular effects, or in building up to a visually effective climax. You unfold a character slowly and by means of dialogue. If you had all the time and paper in the world you could undoubtedly get to your point by using dialogue alone, but, you see, you have space and effectiveness to consider. You'll have to do some of it in straight narrative form. No, all in all, I think we'd better work on your weak spots. You might read a lot of E. M. Forster in your spare time. He gets from point to point remarkably well. In the meanwhile, here's a passage for you to meditate upon. It's from Edith Wharton's *The Writing of Fiction*:

> The use of dialogue in fiction seems to be one of the few things about which a fairly definite rule may be laid down. It should be reserved for the culminating moments, and regarded as the spray into which the great wave of narrative breaks in curving toward the watcher on the shore. This lifting and scattering of the wave, the coruscation of the spray, even the mere material sight of the page broken into short, uneven

paragraphs, all help to reenforce the contrast between such climaxes and the smooth effaced gliding of the narrative intervals; and the contrast enhances that sense of the passage of time for the producing of which the writer has to depend on his intervening narration. Thus the sparing use of dialogue not only serves to emphasize the crises of a tale, but to give it as a whole a greater effect of continuous development.'

Or the exhortation may take the form of remarking a minor stylistic matter, and you will address yourself on it: 'By the way, do you realize that you overwork the word "colorful"? Every time you're in too much of a hurry to find the exact word you want you fall back on that; you're using it to death. Very sloppy habit. In the first place it's, usually, too vaguely inclusive to give the effect you want, and in the second, it is being used by all the advertising writers in the country just now. Stay away from it for a while.'

Be Specific In Suggestions

Although you may not be quite so direct as this in your discourse, still you are advised to address yourself *directly* on these points, making the complaints specific, and, wherever possible, suggesting specific remedies. You will remember more easily, and you will have reenforced your own discontent with this or that element in your writing in such a way that you must take steps to correct the slipshod practice or confess that you are not working seriously at the profession you have chosen. Make a clean-cut issue for yourself wherever you are able to put your finger on a fault; if you suspect that there are weaknesses which you do not see for some reason, show your work to someone whose good taste and judgment you trust. You will often find that a reader who has no pretensions to literary knowledge can put a finger on your stylistic sins as directly as a writer, an editor, or a teacher; but turn to outside counsel only after you have done all you are able to do for yourself. In the long run, it is *your* taste and *your* judgment that must carry you over the pitfalls, and the sooner you educate yourself into being all things to your writing-character the better your prospects are.

Correction After Criticism

Press home all the points on which you have any doubts. Do you use too many short declarative sentences, or too many exclamation points? Is your vocabulary lush, or too severe? Are you so reticent that you slide over an emotional scene so rapidly that your reader may miss the very thing you are trying to convey? Do you indulge in blood-and-thunder past the point of credibility? Then try to find the antidote. The reticent writer can force himself to read Swinburne, or Carlyle, or any one of a number of contemporary authors who are more sensational than decorous. The oversensational can reverse the recommendation and read the eighteenth-century Englishmen, or such writers as William Dean Howells, Willa Cather, Agnes Repplier. If you have a dull and prosy note, a course in the novels and stories of G. K. Chesterton should be of advantage. There is almost no limit to the recommendations which could be made, but you must learn both to diagnose your own case and to find your own best medicine. When you have found your antidote, read with humility, determined to see the excellence in writers who are natively antipathetic to you; while you are performing your stylistic penance, give yourself no quarter. Leave the books which usually attract you severely alone.

The Conditions of Excellence

Next set yourself to discover if you can see any connection between a good morning's work and the conditions of the evening before. Can you tell whether or not the good writing came after you had spent an active day, or after a quiet one? Did you write more easily after going to bed early, or after a short sleep? Is there any observable connection between seeing certain friends and the vividness or dullness of the next morning's work? How did you write on the morning after you had been to a theater, or to an exhibition of pictures, or to a dance? Notice such things, and try to arrange for the type of activity which results in good work.

Dictating a Daily Regime

Then turn your attention to your daily regime. Most writers flourish greatly on a simple, healthy routine with occasional time off for gaiety. Here you will touch the very foundations of prosaic common sense, for you will have to decide on such matters as what diet suits you and what food you must leave alone. If you are going in for a lifetime of writing, it stands to reason that you must learn to work without the continual use of stimulants, so find what ones you can use in moderation and what must be dropped. Bursts of work are not what you are out to establish as your habit, but a good, steady, satisfying flow, rising occasionally to an extraordinary level of performance, but seldom falling below what you have discovered is your own normal output. A completely honest inventory, taken every two or three months, or twice a year at the least, will keep you up to the best and most abundant writing of which you are capable.

While you are having this honest showdown is the time to ask yourself whether you are allowing your temperamental side too much voice in the conduct of your daily life. Do you find yourself emotional and headstrong in situations where an unprejudiced observer would expect you to be dispassionate and judicial? Are you hampering yourself by being resentful or envious or easily depressed? These are all matters to be cleared up by quiet consideration. Envy, depression, resentment, will poison the very springs from which your work flows, and the sooner you eradicate the faintest traces of them the better your writing will be.

When you have these sessions, have them thoroughly. This close, analytical probing of yourself should be done rarely, but well. You must be not only strict with yourself but fair. A blanket condemnation will get you no further than uncritical self-approval. If there is a type of writing which you do well, by all means recognize it and encourage yourself by it. Hold your own good work up to yourself as a standard, and exact work of the same grade in other lines.

After each of these sessions you will see that you emerge with a clearer idea of yourself, your abilities, and your weaknesses. At first you are likely to emphasize some points over others, and later will be astonished at your own blindness to equally important items. But you will have learned how to keep a friendly, critical eye on your own progress, and what steps to take to bring yourself nearer your goal. Once more: don't follow yourself around, nagging and suggesting and complaining. When you feel that you would benefit by an inventory, set an hour for it, have it thoroughly, take the suggestions you have made; then come out and live without introspection till the next occasion for an overhauling arises.

Chapter Nine

READING AS A WRITER

To get the most benefit from the corrective reading you are going to do after these periodical inventories, you must take a little trouble to learn to read as a writer. Anyone who is at all interested in authorship has some sense of every book as a specimen, and not merely as a means of amusement. But to read effectively it is necessary to learn to consider a book in the light of what it can teach you about the improvement of your own work.

Most would-be writers are bookworms, and many of them are fanatical about books and libraries. But there is often a deep distaste at the idea of dissecting a book, or reading it solely for style, or for construction, or to see how its author has handled his problems. Some feeling that one will never again get the bewitched, fascinated interest from any volume that one got as an uncritical but appreciative reader makes many a student-writer protest at the idea of putting his favorite authors under a microscope. As a matter of fact, when you have learned to read critically you will find that your pleasure is far deeper than it was when you read as an amateur; even a bad book becomes tolerable when you are engaged in probing it for the reasons for its stiff, unnatural effects.

Read Twice

At first you will find that the only way to read as a writer is to go over everything twice. Read the story, article, or novel to be studied rapidly and uncritically, as you did in the days when you had no responsibility to a book but to enjoy it. When you have finished put it aside for a while, and take up a pencil and scratch pad.

Summary Judgment and Detailed Analysis

First make a short written synopsis of what you have just read. Now pass a kind of summary judgment on it: you liked it, or didn't like it. You believed it, or were left incredulous. You liked part of it, and disliked the rest. (You may, if you like later, pass a moral judgment on it, too, but now confine your decisions to what you believe were the author's intentions, as far as you are able to discern them.)

Go on to enlarge on these flat statements. If you liked it, why did you? Don't be discouraged if your answer to this is vague at first. You are going to read the book again, and will have another chance to see whether you can find the source of your response. If part of it seemed good to you and the rest weak, see whether you are able to tell when the author lost your assent. Were the characters drawn with uniform skill, badly drawn, or inconsistent only occasionally? Do you know why you felt this?

Do any of the scenes stand out in your mind? Because they were well done, or because an opportunity was so stupidly missed? Remember any passage which arrested your attention for any reason. Is the dialogue natural, or, if stylized, is the formality purposeful or a sign of the author's limitations?

By this time you know some of your own weaknesses. How does the author you have just read handle situations which would be difficult for you?

The Second Reading

If it is a good book your list of questions should be long and searching, your answers particularized as much as possible. If it is not especially good it will be enough, at first, to find the weak spots in it and lay it aside. When you have made your synopsis and answered your own questions as far as possible, make a check against those you were not able to answer fully, or that seem to promise more enlightenment if you pursue them. Now start at the first word again, reading slowly and thoroughly, noting down your answers as they become plain to you. If you find any passage particularly well done, and especially if the author has used adroitly material which would be hard for you to handle, mark them. Later you can return to them and use them as models after further analysis.

You know now how the story ends; be on the watch for the clues to that ending which come early in the book or story. Where was the character trait that brings about the major complication first mentioned? Was it brought in smoothly and subtly, or lugged in by the ears? Do you find, on second reading, that there are false clues – passages which do not make the book more real, or which distort the author's intention, but which have been allowed to pass although they introduce an unnecessary element or actually mislead the reader? Go over such passages carefully, to make sure that *you* are not missing the author's full meaning, and be sure that you are right before concluding that the author was at fault.

Points of Importance

There is no end to the amount of stimulation and help you can get from reading with critical attention. Read with every faculty alert. Notice the rhythm of the book, and whether it is accelerated or slowed when the author wishes to be emphatic. Look for mannerisms and favorite words, and decide for yourself whether they are worth trying for practice or whether they are too plainly the author's own to reward you for learning their structure. How does he get the characters from one scene to another, or mark the passing of time? Does he alter his vocabulary and emphasis when he centers his attention first on one character and then on another? Does he seem to be omniscient, is he telling only what would be apparent to one character and allowing the story to dawn on the reader by following that character's enlightenment? Or does he write first from the viewpoint of one and then another, and then a third? How does he get contrast? Is it, for instance, by placing character against setting incongruously – as Mark Twain put his Connecticut Yankee down into the world of King Arthur's day?

Each writer will ask his own questions and find his own suggestive points. After the first few books – which you *must* read twice if you are to make good use of the work of others – you will find that you can read for enjoyment and for criticism simultaneously, reserving a second reading only for those pages where the author has been at his best or worst.

– Chapter Ten –

ON IMITATION

Now as to imitation for practice. When you have learned to find in the writing of others the material which is suggestive for your own work, you are in a position to imitate in the only way in which imitation can be of any use to you. The philosophies, the ideas, the dramatic notions of other writers of fiction should not be directly adopted. If you find them congenial, go back to the sources from which those authors originally drew their ideas, if you are able to find them. There study the primary sources and take any items over into your own work only when they have your deep acquiescence – never because the author in whose work you find them is temporarily successful, or because another can use them effectively. They are yours to use only when you have made them your own by full acquaintance and acceptance.

Imitating Technical Excellences

But technical excellences can be imitated, and with great advantage. When you have found a passage, long or short, which seems to you far better than anything of the sort you are yet able to do, sit down to learn from it.

Study it even more closely than you have been studying your specimen book or specimen story as a whole. Tear it apart almost word by word. If possible, find a cognate passage in your own work to use for comparison. Let us assume, for instance, that you have trouble with that bugbear of most writers when they first begin to work seriously – conveying the passing of time. You either string out your story to no purpose, following your character through a number of unimportant or confusing activities to get him from one significant scene to another, or you drop him abruptly and take him up abruptly between two paragraphs. In the story you have been reading, which is about the length of the one you want to write, you find that the author has handled such transitions smoothly, writing just enough, but not a word too much, to convey the illusion of time's passing between two scenes. Well, then; how does he do it? He uses – how many words? Absurd as it may seem at first to think that anything can be learned by word-counting, you will soon realize that a good author has a just sense of proportion; he is artist enough to feel how much space should be given to take his character from the thick of action in one situation into the center of the next.

How to Spend Words

In a story of five thousand words, let us say, your author has given a hundred and fifty words to the passing of a night and a day, rather unimportant, in the life of his hero. And you? Three words, or a sentence perhaps: 'The next day, Conrad, etc.'* Something too skimpy about it altogether. Or, on the other hand, although there was nothing in Conrad's night and morning that was pertinent to the story in hand, and although you have already used up all the space you can afford in the sketching of your hero's character, by sheer inability to stop talking about him once you have started you may have given six hundred or a thousand words to the retailing of totally irrelevant matters about his day.

How does the author expend the words that you have counted? Does he drop for a few paragraphs into indirection, after having told the story up to this time straightforwardly? Does he choose words which convey action, in order to show that his hero, although not engaged during that time in anything that furthered the story, still has a full life while he is, as it were, offstage?

---

* I hasten to say that there are occasions on which the words, 'The next day, Conrad, etc.,' may be exactly the number of words and exactly the emphasis to be given to a transition. We are assuming for the moment that such a transition is, for the story you are engaged on, too abrupt.

What clues does he drop into the concluding sentence which allows him to revert to the true action? When you have found as much as you are able to find in that way, write a paragraph of your own, imitating your model *sentence by sentence*.

Counteracting Monotony

Again it may be that you feel that your writing is monotonous, that verb follows noun, and adverb follows verb, with a deadly sameness throughout your pages. You are struck by the variety, the pleasant diversity of sentence structures and rhythms in the author you are reading. Here is the real method of playing the sedulous ape: The first sentence has twelve words; you will write a twelve word sentence. It begins with two words of one syllable each, the third is a noun of two syllables, the fourth is an adjective of four syllables, the fifth an adjective of three, etc. Write one with words of the same number of syllables, noun for noun, adjective for adjective, verb for verb, being sure that the words carry their emphasis on the same syllables as those in the model. By choosing an author whose style is complementary to your own you can teach yourself a great deal about sentence formation and prose rhythm in this way. You will not wish, or need, to do it often, but to do it occasionally is remarkably helpful. You become aware of variation and tone in your reading, and learn as you read. Once having taken the trouble to analyze a sentence into its component parts and construct a similar one of your own, you will find that some part of your mind is thereafter awake to subtleties which you may have passed obliviously before.

Pick Up Fresh Words

Be on the alert to find appropriate words wherever you read, but before you use them be sure they are congruous when side by side with the words of your own vocabulary. Combing a thesaurus for what an old professor of mine used to call, contemptuously, 'vivid verbs' will be far less useful than to find words in the midst of a living story; although a thesaurus is a good tool if it is used as it is meant to be.

Last of all, turn back to your own writing and read it with new eyes: read it as it will look if it makes its way into print. Are there changes you can make which will turn it into effective, diversified, vigorous prose?

– Chapter Eleven –

LEARNING TO SEE AGAIN

The Blinders of Habit

The genius keeps all his days the vividness and intensity of interest that a sensitive child feels in his expanding world. Many of us keep this responsiveness well into adolescence; very few mature men and women are fortunate enough to preserve it in their routine lives. Most of us are only intermittently aware, even in youth, and the occasions on which adults see and feel and hear with every sense alert become rarer and rarer with the passage of years. Too many of us allow ourselves to go about wrapped in our personal problems, walking blindly through our days with our attention all given to some petty matter of no particular importance. The true neurotic may be engrossed in a problem so deeply buried in his being that he could not tell you what it is that he is contemplating, and the sign of his neurosis is his ineffectiveness in the real world. The most normal of us allow ourselves to become so insulated by habit that few things can break through our preoccupations except truly spectacular events – a catastrophe happening under our eyes, our indolent strolling blocked by a triumphal parade; it must be a matter which challenges us in spite of ourselves.

This dullness of apprehension to which we all submit spinelessly is a real danger to a writer. Since we are not laying up for ourselves daily observations, fresh sensations, new ideas, we tend to turn back for our material to the same period in our lives, and write and rewrite endlessly the sensations of our childhood or early years.

Causes of Repetitiousness

Everyone knows an author who seems to have, somehow, only one story to tell. The characters may be given different names from book to book, they may be put into ostensibly different situations; their story may end happily or on a tragic note. Nevertheless we feel each time we read a new book by that author that we have heard the same thing before. Whatever the heroine's name, we can be sure that snowflakes will fall and melt on her eyelashes, or that on a woodland walk her hair will be caught by a twig. A hero of D. H. Lawrence will drop into Lancashire dialect in moments of emotion, a heroine of Storm Jameson is likely to make a success at advertising writing and to have come from a shipbuilding family. Kathleen Norris will give you a blue mixing bowl in a sunny kitchen at least in every other book – and so on, ad infinitum. The temptation to rework material which has an emotional value for us is so great that it is almost never resisted; and there is no reason why it should be, if the reworking is well done. But often one is led to suspect that the episode is used through thoughtlessness and that with a little more trouble the author might have been able to turn up equivalent touches, just as valid, just as effective emotionally, and far less stale. The truth is that we all have a tendency to remember things which we saw under the clear, warm light of childhood, and to return to them whenever we wish to bring a scene to life. But if we continue to use the same episodes and items over and over we lose effectiveness.

Recapturing Innocence of Eye

It is perfectly possible to strip yourself of your preoccupations, to refuse to allow yourself to go about wrapped in a cloak of oblivion day and night, although it is more difficult than one might think to learn to turn one's attention outward again after years of immersion in one's own problems. Merely deciding that you will not be oblivious is hardly enough, although every writer should take the recommendation of Henry James, and register it like a vow: 'Try to be one of the people on

whom nothing is lost.'★ By way of getting to that
desirable state, set yourself a short period each day when
you will, by taking thought, recapture a childlike
'innocence of eye'. For half an hour each day transport
yourself back to the state of wide-eyed interest that was
yours at the age of five. Even though you feel a little
self-conscious about doing something so deliberately
that was once as unnoticed as breathing, you will still
find that you are able to gather stores of new material
in a short time. Don't plan to use the material at once,
for you may get only the brittle, factual little items of
the journalist if you do not wait for the unconscious
mind to work its miracles of assimilation and accretion
on them. But turn yourself into a stranger in your own
streets.

A Stranger in the Streets

You know how vividly you see a strange town or a
strange country when you first enter it. The huge red
buses careening through London, on the wrong side of
the road to every American that ever saw them – soon
they are as easy to dodge and ignore as the green buses
of New York, and as little wonderful as the drugstore
window that you pass on your way to work each day.
The drugstore window, though, the streetcar that
carries you to work, the crowded subway, can look as

★ In his essay 'The Art of Fiction,' in *Partial Portraits*. Macmillan.

strange as Xanadu if you refuse to take them for granted. As you get into your streetcar, or walk along a street, tell yourself that for fifteen minutes you will notice and tell yourself about every single thing that your eyes rest on. The streetcar: what color is it outside? (Not just green or red, here, but sage or olive green, scarlet or maroon.) Where is the entrance? Has it a conductor and motorman, or a motorman-conductor in one? What colors inside, the walls, the floor, the seats, the advertising posters? How do the seats face? Who is sitting opposite you? How are your neighbors dressed, how do they stand or sit, what are they reading, or are they sound asleep? What sounds are you hearing, what smells are reaching you, how does the strap feel under your hand, or the stuff of the coat that brushes past you? After a few moments you can drop your intense awareness, but plan to resume it again when the scene changes.

Another time speculate on the person opposite you. What did she come from, and where is she going? What can you guess about her from her face, her attitude, her clothes? What, do you imagine, is her home like?*

It will be worth your while to walk on strange streets, to visit exhibitions, to hunt up a movie in a strange part of town in order to give yourself the experience of fresh seeing once or twice a week. But

* See the story entitled 'An Unwritten Novel' in Virginia Woolf's *Monday or Tuesday*.

any moment of your life can be used, and the room that you spend most of your waking hours in is as good, or better, to practice responsiveness on as a new street. Try to see your home, your family, your friends, your school or office, with the same eyes that you use away from your own daily route. There are voices you have heard so often that you forget they have a timbre of their own; unless you are morbidly hypersensitive, the chances are that you hardly realize that your best friend has a tendency to use some words so frequently that if you were to write a sentence involving those words anyone who knew him would realize whom you were imitating.

All such easy and minor exercises are excellent for you if you really want to write. No one cares to follow a dull and stodgy mind through innumerable pages, and a mind is so easily freshened. Remember that part of the advice is to put what you notice *into definite words* before you abandon it to the manipulation of the unconscious. Finding the exact words is not always necessary, but much usable stuff will slip through your fingers if you do not emphasize it in this way. If you think, 'Oh, I'm sure to remember that,' you will find that you are often merely begging off from a hard task. You aren't finding the words for the new sensation simply because the words do not come easily; persistently going after the right phrase will reward you with a striking, well-realized item sometime when you need it badly.

The Rewards of Virtue

Shortly after you begin looking about you like this you will see that your morning's pages are fuller and better than before. It is not only that you are bringing new material to them every day, but you are stirring the latent memories in your mind. Each fresh fact starts a train of associations reaching down into the depths of your nature, releasing for your use sensations and experiences, old delights, old sorrows, days that have been overlaid in your memory, episodes which you had quite forgotten.

This is one reason for the inexhaustible resources of the true genius. Everything that ever happened to him is his to use. No experience is so deeply buried that he cannot revive it; he can find a type-episode for every situation that his imagination can present. By the simple means of refusing to let yourself fall into indifference and boredom, you can reach and revive for your writing every aspect of your life.

Chapter Twelve

THE SOURCE OF ORIGINALITY

It is a commonplace that every writer must turn to himself to find most of his material; it is such a commonplace that a chapter on the subject is likely to be greeted with groans. Nevertheless it must be written, for only a thorough understanding of the point will clear away the misapprehensions as to what constitutes 'originality.'

The Elusive Quality

Every book, every editor, every teacher will tell you that the great key to success in authorship is originality. Beyond that they seldom go. Sometimes they will point out to the persistent inquirer someone whose work shows the 'originality' that they require, and those free examples are often responsible for some of the direst mistakes that young writers fall into. 'Be original, like William Faulkner,' an editor will say, meaning only to enforce his advice by an instance; or ' Look at Mrs Buck; now if you could give me something like that – !' And the earnest inquirer, quite missing the point of the exhortation, goes home and tries with all his might to turn out what I have already complained of: 'a marvelous Faulkner story,' or 'a perfect Pearl Buck novel.' Once in a long while – a very long while, if my experience as editor and teacher counts for anything – the imitative writer actually finds in his model some quality so congenial that he is able to turn out an acceptable story on the same pattern. But for one who succeeds there are hundreds who fail. I could find it in my heart to wish that everyone who cut his coat by another man's pattern would find the result a crass failure. For originality does not lie down that road.

It is well to understand as early as possible in one's writing life that there is just one contribution which every one of us can make: we can give into the common pool of experience some comprehension of the world as it looks to each of us. There is one sense in which everyone is unique. No one else was born of your parents, at just that time of just that country's history; no one underwent just your experiences, reached just your conclusions, or faces the world with the exact set of ideas that you must have. If you can come to such friendly terms with yourself that you are able and willing to say precisely what you think of any given situation or character, if you can tell a story as it can appear only to you of all the people on earth, you will inevitably have a piece of work which is original.

Now this, which seems so simple, is the very thing that the average writer cannot do. Partly because he has immersed himself in the writing of others since he was able to read at all, he is sadly apt to see the world through someone else's eyes. Occasionally, being imaginative and pliable, he does a very good job of it, and we have a story which is near enough to an original story to seem good, or not to show too plainly that it is derivative. But often those faults in comprehension, those sudden misunderstandings of one's own fictional characters, come from the fact that the author is not looking at the persons of his own creation with his own eyes; he is using the eyes of Mr Faulkner, of Mr Hemingway, of D. H. Lawrence or Mrs Woolf.

Originality Not Imitation

The virtue of those writers is precisely that they have refused to do what their imitators do so humbly. Each of them has had a vision of the world and has set out to transcribe it, and their work has the forthrightness and vigor of all work that comes from the central core of the personality without deviation or distortion. There is always a faint flavor of humbug about a Dreiserian story written by some imitator of Mr Dreiser, or one of those stark mystical Laurentian tales not directly fathered by D. H. Lawrence; but it is exceedingly hard to persuade the timid or hero-worshipping young writer that this must always be so.

The 'Surprise Ending'

When the pitfall of imitation is safely skirted, one often finds that in the effort to be original an author has pulled and jerked and prodded his story into monstrous form. He will plant dynamite at its crisis, turn the conclusion inside out, betray a character by making him act uncharacteristically, all in the service of the God of Originals. His story may be all compact of horror, or, more rarely, good luck may conquer every obstacle hands down; and if the teacher or editor protests that the story has not been made credible, its author will murmur '*Dracula*' or 'Kathleen Norris,' and will be unconvinced if told that the minimum requirement for a good story has not been met: that he has not shown that he, the author, truly and consistently envisages a world in which such events could under any circumstances come to pass, as the authors whom he is imitating certainly do.

Honesty, the Source of Originality

So these stories fail from their own inconsistency, although the author has at his command, in the mere exercise of stringent honesty, the best source of consistency for his own work. If you can discover what you are like, if you can discover what you truly believe about most of the major matters of life, you will be able to write a story which is honest and original and unique. But those are very large 'ifs,' and it takes hard digging to get at the roots of one's own convictions.

Very often one finds a beginner who is unwilling to commit himself because he knows just enough about his own processes to be sure that his beliefs of today are not likely to be his beliefs of tomorrow. This operates to hold him under a sort of spell. He waits for final wisdom to arrive, and since it tarries he feels that he cannot commit himself in print. When this is a real difficulty, and not simply (as it sometimes is) a neurotic excuse to postpone writing indefinitely, you will find a writer who can turn out a sketch, a half-story with no commitments in it, but seldom more. Obviously what such a writer needs is to be made to realize that his case is not isolated; that we all continue to grow, and that in order to write at all we must write on the basis of our present beliefs. If you are unwilling to write from the honest, though perhaps far from final, point of view that represents your present state, you may come to your deathbed with your contribution to the world still unmade, and just as far from final conviction about the universe as you were at the age of twenty.

Trust Yourself

There are only so many dramatic situations in which man can find himself – three dozen, if one is to take seriously *The Thirty-six Dramatic Situations* of Georges Polti – and it is not the putting of your character in the central position of a drama which has never been dreamed of before that will make your story irresistible. Even if it were possible to find such a situation it would be an almost heartbreaking feat to communicate it to your readers, who must find some recognizable quality in the story they read or be hopelessly at sea. How *your* hero meets his dilemma, what *you* think of the impasse – those are the things which make your story truly your own; and it is your own individual character, unmistakably showing through your work, which will lead you to success or failure. I would almost be willing to go so far as to say that there is no situation which is trite in itself, there are only dull, unimaginative, or uncommunicative authors. No dilemma in which a man can find himself will leave his fellows unmoved if it can be fully presented. There is, for instance, a recognizable thematic likeness between *The Way of All Flesh*, *Clayhanger*, and *Of Human Bondage*. Which of them is trite?

'Your Anger and My Anger'

Agnes Mure MacKenzie, in *The Process of Literature*, says, 'Your loving and my loving, your anger and my anger, are sufficiently alike for us to be able to call them by the same names: but in our experience and in that of any two people in the world, they will never be quite completely identical'; if that were not literally true there would be neither basis nor opportunity for art. And again, in a recent issue of the *Atlantic Monthly*, Mrs Wharton, writing *The Confessions of a Novelist*, declares: 'As a matter of fact, there are only two essential rules: one, that the novelist should deal only with what is within his reach, literally or figuratively (in most cases the two are synonymous), and the other that the value of a subject depends almost wholly on what the author sees in it, and how deeply he is able to see into it.'

By returning to those quotations from time to time you may at last persuade yourself that it is your insight which gives the final worth to your writing, and that there is no triteness where there is a good, clear, honest mind at work.

One Story, Many Versions

Very early in my classes I set out to prove this by direct demonstration. I ask for synopses of stories reduced to the very bones of an outline. Of those that are offered I choose the 'tritest.' In one class this was offered: 'A spoiled girl marries and nearly ruins her husband by her attitude toward money.' I confess that when I read this aloud to my pupils my heart misgave me. I could foresee, myself, only one elaboration of it, with one possible variation which would only occur to those who could perform the rather sophisticated feat of 'dissociation' upon it – those, that is, who could discover what their immediate response to the idea was, and then deliberately alter their first association into its opposite. The class was asked to write for ten minutes, expanding the sentence into a paragraph or two, as if they were going to write a story on the theme. The result, in a class of twelve members, was twelve versions so different from each other that any editor could have read them all on the same day without realizing that the point of departure was the same in each.

We had, to begin with, a girl who was spoiled because she was a golf champion, and who, since she was an amateur, nearly ruined her husband by traveling around to tournaments. We had a story of a politician's daughter who had entertained her father's possible supporters and who entertained her husband's employer too lavishly, leading him to think that his young right-hand man was too sure of promotion. We had a story of a girl who had been warned that young wives were usually too extravagant, and who consequently pinched and pared and cut corners till she wore out her husband's patience. Before the second variation was half-read the class was laughing outright. Each member realized that she, too, had seen the situation in some purely personal light, and that what seemed so inevitable to her was fresh and unforeseen to the others. I wish I could conclude this anecdote by saying that I never again heard one of them complain that the only idea she could think of was too platitudinous to use, but this story really happened.

Nevertheless it is true that not even twins will see the same story idea from the same angle. There will always be differences of emphasis, a choice of different factors to bring about the dilemma and different actions to solve it. If you can once believe this thoroughly you can release for your immediate use any idea which has enough emotional value to engage your attention at all. If you find yourself groping for a theme you may take this as a fair piece of advice, simple as it sounds: 'You can write about anything which has been vivid enough to cause you to comment upon it.' If a situation has caught your attention to that extent, it has meaning for you, and if you can find what that meaning is you have the basis for a story.

Your Inalienable Uniqueness

Every piece of writing which is not simply the purveying of straightforward information – as a recipe or a formula is, for example – is an essay in persuasion. You are persuading your reader, while you hold his attention, to see the world with your eyes, to agree with you that this is a stirring occasion, that that situation is essentially tragic, or that another is deeply humorous. All fiction is persuasive in this sense. The author's conviction underlies all imaginative representation of whatever grade.

Since this is so, it behooves you to know what you do believe of most of the major problems of life, and of those minor problems which you are going to use in your writing.

A Questionnaire

Here are a few questions for a self-examination which may suggest others to you. It is by no means an exhaustive questionnaire, but by following down the other inquiries which occur to you as you consider these, you can come by a very fair idea of your working philosophy:

Do you believe in a God? Under what aspect? (Hardy's 'President of the Immortals,' Wells' 'emerging God'?)

Do you believe in free will or are you a determinist? (Although an artist-determinist is such a walking paradox that imagination staggers at the notion.)

Do you like men? Women? Children?

What do you think of marriage?

Do you consider romantic love a delusion and a snare?

Do you think the comment 'It will all be the same in a hundred years' is profound, shallow, true or false?

What is the greatest happiness you can imagine? The greatest disaster?

And so on. If you find that you are balking at definite answers to the great questions, then you are not yet ready to write fiction which involves major issues. You must find subjects on which you are capable of making up your mind, to serve as the groundwork of your writing. The best books emerge from the strongest convictions – and for confirmation see any bookshelf.

– Chapter Thirteen –

THE WRITER'S RECREATION

Authors are more given than any other tribe to the taking of busmen's holidays. In their off-hours they can usually be found reading in a corner, or, if thwarted in that, with other writers, talking shop. A certain amount of shoptalk is valuable; too much of it is a drain. And too much reading is very bad indeed.

Busmen's Holidays

All of us, whether we follow writing as a career or not, are so habituated to words that we cannot escape them. If we are left alone long enough and forbidden to read, we will very soon be talking to ourselves – 'subvocally' as the behaviorists say. This is the easiest thing in the world to prove: starve yourself for a few hours in a wordless void. Stay alone, and resist the temptation to take up any book, paper, or scrap of printed matter that you can find; also flee the temptation to telephone someone when the strain begins to make itself felt – for you will almost surely scheme internally to be reading or talking within a few minutes. In a very short while you will find that you are using words at a tremendous rate: planning to tell an acquaintance just what you think of him, examining your conscience and giving yourself advice, trying to recapture the words of a song, turning over the plot of a story; in fact, words have rushed in to fill the wordless vacuum.

Prisoners who never wrote a word in the days of their freedom will write on any paper they can lay hands on. Innumerable books have been begun by patients lying on hospital beds, sentenced to silence and refused reading; the last one to be reported was, I think, Margaret Ayer Barnes' *Years of Grace*, and long ago I remember reading that William Allen White's *A Certain Rich Man* came to him when he was 'tossing pebbles into the sea' on an enforced vacation. A two-year-old will tell himself stories, and a farmer will talk to a cow. Once we have learned to use words we must be forever using them.

Wordless Recreation

The conclusion should be plain. If you want to stimulate yourself into writing, amuse yourself in wordless ways. Instead of going to a theater, hear a symphony orchestra, or go by yourself to a museum; go alone for long walks, or ride by yourself on a bus-top. If you will conscientiously refuse to talk or read you will find yourself compensating for it to your great advantage.

One very well-known writer of my acquaintance sits for two hours a day on a park bench. He says that for years he used to lie on the grass of his back garden and stare at the sky, but some member of the family, seeing him so conveniently alone and aimless, always seized the occasion to come out and sit beside him for a nice talk. Sooner or later, he himself would begin to talk about the work he had in mind, and, to his astonishment, he discovered that the urgent desire to write the story disappeared as soon as he had got it thoroughly talked out. Now, with a purposeful air and in mysterious silence, he disappears daily, and can be found every afternoon (but fortunately seldom is) with his hands in his pockets staring at the pigeons in the park.

Another writer, almost tone-deaf, says that she can finish any story she starts if she can find a hall where a long symphony is being played. The lights, the music, her immobility, bring on a sort of artistic coma, and she emerges in a sleepwalking state which lasts till she reaches the typewriter.

Find Your Own Stimulus

Only experiment will show you what your own best recreation is; but books, the theater, and talking pictures should be very rarely indulged in when you have any piece of writing to finish. The better the book or the play is the more likely it is, not only to distract you, but actually to alter your mood, so that you return to your own writing with your attitude changed.

A Variety of Time-Fillers

Most established authors have some way of silent recreation. One found that horseback riding was the best relaxation for him; another, a woman, confessed that whenever she came to a difficult spot in a novel she was writing, she got up and played endless games of solitaire. (I believe it was Mrs Norris, and I think she went so far as to say that she was not always certain to see an ace when she turned it up.) Another woman novelist found, during the war years, that she spun stories as fast as she knitted, and turned herself into a Penelope of the knitting needle, raveling a square of scarlet wool and starting on it again whenever she had a story 'simmering.' Fishing served a writer of detective stories, and another admits that he whittles aimlessly for hours. Still another said that she embroidered initials on everything she could lay her hands on.

Only an impassioned author could call some of these occupations by any name so glamorous as 'recreation'; but it is to be noticed that successful writers, when talking about themselves *as writers*, say little about curling up in a corner with a good book. Much as they may love reading (and all authors would rather read than eat), they had all learned from long experience that it is the wordless occupation which sets their own minds busily at work.

– Chapter Fourteen –

THE PRACTICE STORY

A Recapitulation

When you have succeeded for some weeks in rising early and writing, and in the second step of going off by yourself at a given moment and beginning to write, you are ready to combine the two; and you are within measurable distance of being ready for the key procedure which every successful artist knows. Why it is kept such a secret, and why it should take a different form in almost every writer, is a mystery. Perhaps because each worked it out for himself and so hardly realizes that it is a part of his special knowledge. But that is matter for another chapter. Now it is time to bring together the work of the conscious and unconscious in an elementary manner.

You were warned not to reread your own work before starting on each morning's writing. You were to try to tap the unconscious directly, not simply to call up from it by way of association a certain limited set of ideas; and, further, if you were to find your own stride it was necessary to free you from the hampering effects of having any example before your eyes. A newspaper a novel the speech of someone else, or even your own writing so long as you are under the influence of others – all have a circumscribing effect. We are very easily drawn into a circle of ideas; we fall into the rhythm of any book or newspaper we read.

The Contagiousness of Style

If you seriously doubt this, it is very easy to demonstrate how one can be caught up into the current of another's style. Choose any writer whose work has a strong rhythm, a decided personal style: Dickens, Thackeray, Kipling, Hemingway, Aldous Huxley, Mrs Wharton, Wodehouse – anyone you like. Read your author until you feel a little fatigue, the first momentary flagging of attention. Put the book aside and write a few pages on any subject. Then compare those pages with the writing you have done in the early morning. You will find a definite difference between the two. You have insensibly altered your own emphasis and inflection in the direction of the author's in whom you have been engrossed. Sometimes the similarity is so striking as to be almost ludicrous, although you intended no parody – may even have intended to write as independently as possible. We can leave it to the psychologists to discover that this is so, and to explain why it should be.

Find Your Own Style

The important matter is to find your own style, your own subjects, your own rhythm, so that every element in your nature can contribute to the work of making a writer of you. Study your own pages; among them you are to find some idea – preferably, this time, a fairly simple one – which offers you a good, obvious nucleus for a short story, an expanded anecdote (say, of *The New Yorker*'s style), or a brief essay. Story material will be best. Anything that is there in your early morning work has real value for you. You will have something to say on the subject which is more than superficial comment. Abstract your idea from its too discursive setting and get down to the matter of considering it seriously.

The Story in Embryo

What shall you make of it? Remember, you are to look for a simple idea – something that can be finished in one sitting. Then, in that case, what will it need? Emphasis? Characters to embody in concrete form the speculations you have made in your sleepy state? Does it need to have certain factors made very plain, so that the conflict, whatever it is, runs no danger of seeming unimportant or of being overlooked? When you have decided what can and should be made of it, consider the details with care.

The Preparatory Period

Mind you, you are not yet to write it. The work you are doing on it is preliminary. For a day or two you are going to immerse yourself in these details; you are going to think about them consciously, turning if necessary to books of reference to fill in your facts. Then you are going to dream about it. You are going to think of the characters separately, then in combination. You are going to do everything you can for that story by using alternately your conscious intelligence and unconscious reverie on it. There will seem no end to the stuff that you can find to work over. What does the heroine look like? Was she an only child, or the eldest of seven? How was she educated? Does she work? Now perform the same labor on the hero, and on any secondary characters you need to bring the story to life. Then turn your attention to the scene, and to those background scenes in each character's life which you may never need to write of, but a knowledge of which will make your finished story that much more convincing.★

★ In his latest book, *It Was the Nightingale*, Ford Madox Ford says, on just this point: 'I may – and quite frequently do – plan out every scene, sometimes even every conversation, in a novel before I sit down to write it. But unless I know the history back to the remotest times of any place of which I am going to write I cannot begin the work. And I must know – from personal observation, not reading, the shapes of windows, the nature of doorknobs, the aspect of kitchens, the material

When you have done everything you can in this way, say to yourself. 'At ten o'clock on Wednesday I will begin to write it,' and then dismiss it from your mind. Now and then it will rise to the surface. You need not reject it with violence, but reject it. You are not ready for it yet; let it subside again. Three days will do it no harm, will even help it. But when ten o'clock strikes on Wednesday you sit down to work.

Writing Confidently

Now; strike out at once. Just as you made yourself do the time exercises in the sixth chapter, take no excuses, refuse to feel any stage fright; simply start working. If a good first sentence does not come, leave a space for it and write it in later. Write as rapidly as possible, with as little attention to your own processes as you can give. Try to work lightly and quickly, beginning and ending each sentence with a good, clear stroke. Reread very little – only a sentence or two now and then to be sure you are on the true course.

In this way you can train yourself into good, workmanlike habits. The typewriter or the writing pad should not appear to you a good place to lose yourself

---

of which dresses are made, the leather used in shoes, the method used in manuring fields, the nature of bus tickets. I shall never use any of these things in the book. But unless I know what sort of doorknob his fingers closed on how shall I – satisfactorily to myself – get my character out of doors?' This book will be found full of valuable sidelights on the process of literature.

in musing, or to work out matters you should have cleared up before. You may find it very helpful, before you begin to write, to settle on a first and last sentence for your story. Then you can use the first sentence as a springboard from which to dive into your work, and the last as a raft to swim toward.

A Finished Experiment

The exercise must end with a completed piece of work, no matter how long you labor at it. Later you will learn how to do writing which cannot be finished at a sitting; the best way is to make another engagement with yourself before you rise from the typewriter, and while the heat of work is still on you. You will find if you do this that you will come to meet yourself, as it were, in the same mood, and there will not be a noticeable alteration in the manner of your writing between one session and the next. But this story is to be finished on the day you begin it.

Whether or not you are going to like it when you read it later, whether or not you decide that you can do a better version of it if you try again, the exercise is not done properly unless you rise from the session with a complete practice story.

Time for Detachment

Put it away, and if your curiosity will let you, leave it alone for two or three days. At the very least let it stay unread overnight. Your judgment on it until you have slept is worth exactly nothing. One of two states of mind will interfere with any earlier appraisal. If you belong to one half the writing race, you will be worn and discouraged, and, reading your own story over with fatigue clouding every line, you will think it the dullest, most improbable, flattest tale ever told. Even if you reread it more favorably later when you are freshened by sleep and diversion, a memory of that first verdict is likely to cause you to wonder which of the judgments is right. And if the story is rejected by the first editor who sees it, you are likely to think that it is as bad as you feared, and you may refuse to give it another chance.

The other half of the brotherhood seems not to use up the last ounce of its energy in getting a story to its close. They, on reading their recent effort, will be still held by the impulse which set them writing in the first place. If they have fallen into errors of judgment, if they have been too verbose or compact, the same astigmatism that was responsible for the mistake in the first place will still operate to blind them to it.

You are simply not ready to read your story objectively when it is newly finished; and there are writers who cannot trust their objectivity toward their own work much under a month. So put it away and turn your attention to something else. Now is the time of times for the reading which you have been denying yourself. Your story is safely written, and will preserve the marks of your personality so tenaciously that not the deepest admiration for the work of another writer will be likely to endanger it. If even reading seems too great an effort, find some mild relaxation which takes your attention quite away from authorship. If you can make a definite break in your routine just here, so much the better. Some writers have an immediate impulse to begin work on another story; if you feel it, by all means give in to it. But if you feel that you never want to see paper and typewriter again, indulge yourself in that mood, too.

The Critical Heading

When you are refreshed, relaxed, and detached, take out your story and read it.

The chances are that you will find a great deal more in your manuscript than you are conscious of having put there. Something was at work for you while you wrote. Scenes which you thought absolutely vital to the proper telling of the story are not there at all; other scenes which you had not planned to write take their places. The characters have traits you had hardly realized. They have said things you had not thought of having them say. Here is a sentence cleverly emphasized which you had thought of as only a casual statement, but which needed that emphasis if the story was to be shapely. In short, you have written both less and more than you intended. Your conscious mind had less to do with it, your unconscious mind more, than you would have believed possible.

Chapter Fifteen

THE GREAT DISCOVERY

The Five-Finger Exercises of Writing

Now those are the five-finger exercises of writing. To recapitulate before we go further, for you can hardly hear too often these primary truths about your art, the writer (like every artist) is a dual personality. In him the unconscious flows freely. He has trained himself so that the physical effort of writing does not tire him out of all proportion to the effect he achieves. His intellect directs, criticizes, and discriminates wherever two possible courses present themselves, in such a way as to leave the more sensitive element of his nature free to bring forth its best fruit. He learns to use his intellect both cursively, as he works, and later, as he considers what he has done during the period of the creative flow. He replaces by conscious intention, and day by day, the drains made on his funds of images, sensations, and ideas, by keeping awake to new observations. Ideally, the two sides of his nature are at peace with each other and work in harmony; at the least he must be able to suppress one or the other at discretion. Each side of his character must learn to be able to trust the other to do what is in its field and to carry the full responsibility for its own work. He restrains each side of his mind to its own functions, never allowing the conscious to usurp the privilege of the unconscious, and vice versa.

Now we go a little more deeply into the contribution of the unconscious, and the piece of writing you have just finished is your laboratory specimen. If you have worked according to instructions, foreseeing as many of the points of your story as you were able to, if you thought and daydreamed about the story without beginning to write prematurely; if then when you had promised yourself to write you got straight to work without hesitation or apology, it is very nearly certain that the resulting piece of writing will be both shapelier and fuller than you could have expected. The story will be balanced in a way which seems more adroit than you would have believed possible. The characters will be more fully, more expertly drawn, and at the same time drawn with more economy, than if you had labored at them with all your conscious mind in action. In short, a faculty has been at work which so far we have hardly considered. The higher imagination, you may call it; your own endowment of genius, great or small; the creative aspect of your mind, which is lodged almost entirely in the unconscious.

The Root of Genius

For the root of genius is in the unconscious, not the conscious, mind. It is not by weighing, balancing, trimming, expanding with conscious intention, that an excellent piece of art is born. It takes its shape and has its origin outside the region of the conscious intellect. There is much that the conscious can do, but it cannot provide you with genius, or with the talent that is genius' second cousin.

Unconscious, Not Subconscious

But we are badly handicapped when we come to talk or write of it, for the mind is not yet fully explored. And there is an even more serious difficulty to be encountered. When the Freudian psychology first reached us, we began to hear, unfortunately for us, about the *sub*conscious. Freud himself has corrected that error in terminology, and it is the *un*conscious that is now mentioned in the canonical works. But for most of us, that unlucky 'sub' carried a derogatory connotation, and we have not entirely freed ourselves from the idea that the unconscious is, in some way, a less laudable part of our makeup than our conscious mind. F.W.H. Myers, in his excellent chapter on 'Genius' in *Human Personality* (which should be read by every prospective author), fell subject to the same temptation and spoke continually of the 'subliminal uprush'. Now the unconscious is not, in its entirety, either below or less than the conscious mind. It includes in its scope everything which is not in the forefront of our consciousness, and has a reach as far above our average intellect as it has depths below.

The Higher Imagination

This spatial terminology is also unfortunate. The thing to realize is that the unconscious must be trusted to bring you aid from a higher level than that on which you ordinarily function. Any art must draw on this higher content of the unconscious as well as on the memories and emotions stored away there. A sound and gifted person is one who draws on and uses continually these resources, who lives in peace and amity with all the reaches of his being; not one who suppresses, at the cost of infinite energy and vitality, every echo from the far region.

Come to Terms with the Unconscious

The unconscious should not be thought of as a limbo where vague, cloudy, and amorphous notions swim hazily about. There is every reason to believe, on the contrary, that it is the great home of form; that it is quicker to see types, patterns, purposes, than our intellect can ever be. Always, it is true, you must be on the watch lest a too heady exuberance sweep you away from a straight course; always you must direct and control the excess of material which the unconscious will offer. But if you are to write well you must come to terms with the enormous and powerful part of your nature which lies behind the threshold of immediate knowledge.

If you can learn to do this, you have less tiring, difficult labor to perform than you believed you had when you first turned to writing. There is a great field of technical knowledge which the writer can study, many shortcuts to effectiveness which can be learned by taking thought. Yet on the whole it is the unconscious which will decide on both the form and the matter of the work which you are planning, and which will, if you can learn to rely on it, give you a far better and more convincing result if you are not continually meddling with its processes and imposing on it your own notions of the plausible, the desirable, the persuasive, according to some formula which you have painstakingly extracted from a work on the technique of fiction, or laboriously plotted out for yourself from long study of stories in print.

The Artistic Coma and the Writer's Magic

The true genius may live his life long without ever realizing how he works. He will know only that there are times when he must, at all costs, have solitude; time to dream, to sit idle. Often he himself believes that his mind is empty. Sometimes we hear of gifted men who are on the verge of despair because they feel they are going through a 'barren' period; but suddenly the time of silence is past, and they have reached the moment when they must write. That strange, aloof, detached period has been called 'the artistic coma' by observers shrewd enough to see that the idleness is only a surface stillness. *Something* is at work, but so deeply and wordlessly that it hardly gives a sign of its activity till it is ready to externalize its vision. The necessity which the artist feels to indulge himself in solitude, in rambling leisure, in long speechless periods, is behind most of the charges of eccentricity and boorishness that are leveled at men of genius. If the period is recognized and allowed for, it need not have a disruptive effect. The artist will always be marked by occasional periods of detachment; the nameless faculty will always announce itself by an air of withdrawal and indifference, but it is possible to hasten the period somewhat, and to have it, to a limited extent, under one's control. To be able to induce at will the activity of that higher imagination, that intuition, that artistic level of the unconscious – that is where the artist's magic lies, and is his only true 'secret.'

Chapter Sixteen

THE THIRD PERSON, GENIUS

The Writer Not Dual But Triple

So, almost insensibly, one arrives at the understanding that the writer's nature is not dual but triple. The third member of the partnership is – feeble or strong, constantly or spasmodically showing – one's individual endowment of genius. The flashes of insight, the penetrating intuitions, the imagination which combines and transmutes ordinary experience into 'the illusion of a higher reality' – all these necessities of art, or, on a humbler level, all these necessities of any interpretation of life, come from a region beyond those we have been studying and learning to control. For most practical purposes it is enough to divide our minds roughly into conscious and unconscious; it is quite possible to live a lifetime (even the lifetime of an artist) without even so much comprehension of the mind's complexity. Yet by recognizing this third component of your nature, by understanding its importance to your writing, by learning to liberate it, to clear obstructions from its path so that it may flow unimpeded into your work, you perform the most vital service of which you are capable to yourself as a writer.

The Mysterious Faculty

Now you begin to see the basis of truth for that discouraging statement, 'Genius cannot be taught.' In a sense, of course, that is the literal truth; but the implications are almost entirely misleading. You cannot add one grain to this faculty by all your conscious efforts, but there is no reason why you should desire to. Its resources at the feeblest are fuller than you can ever exhaust. What we need is not to add to that natural endowment, but to learn to use it. The great men of every period and race – so great that we call them, for simplicity's sake, by the name of that one faculty alone, as though in them it existed with no admixture, the 'geniuses' – are those who were able to free more of that faculty for use in their lives and in their works of art than the rest of mankind. No human being is so poor as to have no trace of genius; none so great that he comes within infinity of using his own inheritance to the full.

The average man fears, distrusts, ignores, or knows nothing of that element of his nature. In moments of deep emotion, in danger, in joy, occasionally when long sickness has quieted the body and the mind, sometimes in a remote, dim apprehension which we bring back with us from sleep, or from moments under an anesthetic, everyone has intimations of it. Traces of it may be seen at its most unmistakable and mysterious in the lives of the prodigies of music.* However mysterious and incomprehensible it is, it exists; and it is no more 'an infinite capacity for taking pains' – as the old definition of genius would have it – than 'inspiration is perspiration'; a pure American delusion if ever there was one. The process of transmitting one's intuitive knowledge, of conveying one's insight at all satisfactorily, may be infinitely laborious. Years may be spent finding the words to set forth the illumination of a moment. But to confuse the labor with the genius that instigated it is to be misled. When one learns to release this faculty even inexpertly, or when it is released fortuitously, one finds that so far from having to toil anxiously and painstakingly for his effects one experiences, on the contrary, the miracle of being carried along on the creative current.

Releasing Genius

Often the release does come accidentally. It is possible for an artist to count on the energy from this region to carry out a book, story, a picture, and yet never

---

* Read any account of Mozart's life, for example.

recognize it. He may even go so far as to deny that any such thing as 'genius' is in question. He will assure you that, in his experience, it is all a matter of 'getting into his stride'; but what getting into his stride implies he may never know, even though in that happy state he writes pages of clarity and beauty beyond anything of which he is capable in his pedestrian moments. Another may, in a burst of candor, tell you that after mulling an idea over till his head aches he comes to a kind of dead end: he can no longer think about his story or even understand why it once appealed to him. Much later, when he is least expecting it, the idea returns, mysteriously rounded and completed, ready for transcribing. And so on. Most successful writers arrive at their own method of releasing this faculty by a trial-and-error process, so obscure that they can seldom offer a beginner in search of the secret so much as a rule-of-thumb. Their reports of their writing habits are so at variance with each other that it is no wonder the young writer sometimes feels that his elders are all engaged in a conspiracy to delude and mislead him as to the actual process of literature.

Rhythm, Monotony, Silence

There is no conspiracy; there is, I should say, remarkably little jealousy or personal envy between writers. They will tell you what they can, but the more instinctively they are artists the less they are able to analyze their ways of working. What one finally gets, after long crossquestionings, after raking through reports, is no explanation, but usually simple statements of personal experience. They agree in reporting that the idea of a book or story is usually apprehended in a flash. At that moment many of the characters, many of the situations, the story's outcome, all may be – either dimly or vividly – prefigured. Then there is a period of intensive thinking and working over of the ideas. With some authors this is a period of great excitement; they seem intoxicated with the possibilities there before their minds. Later comes a quiescent period; and since almost every writer alive occupies himself in some quite idiosyncratic way in that interlude, it is seldom noticed that these occupations have a kind of common denominator. Horseback riding; knitting; shuffling and dealing cards; walking; whittling; you see they *have* a common denominator – of three figures, one might say. All these occupations are rhythmical, monotonous, and wordless. And that is our key.

In other words, every author, in some way which he has come on by luck or long search, puts himself into a very light state of hypnosis. The attention is held, but *just* held; there is no serious demand on it. Far behind the mind's surface, so deep that he is seldom aware (unless at last observation of himself has taught him) that any activity is going forward, his story is being fused and welded into an integrated work.

A Floor to Scrub

With no more clue than that you might be able to find some such occupation of your own; or you may recognize in some recurrent habit the promise of an occupation which would be useful to you. But the disadvantage of most of these accidentally discovered time-fillers is that they are only rude expedients. When they *have* been found they are seldom abandoned. Indeed, many writers reach a state of real superstition about the method which has worked for them. 'I'd be all right if I had a floor to scrub,' one of my pupils said to me, a professor's wife who had written in the intervals of bringing up a large family, and had found that her stories fell into line best when she was at work on the kitchen floor. A little success had brought her to the city to study; she convinced herself completely that she would be unable to write again till she got back to the rhythmical monotony of the scrubbing brush. This is an extreme case; but there are many famous authors with superstitions just as stubbornly and firmly, although less outspokenly, held as my middle-western house-mother's. And indeed most of the methods which have been discovered accidentally are as arbitrary, wasteful, and haphazard as scrubbing floors.

There is a way to shorten that 'incubating period' and produce a better piece of work. And that way is the writer's magic which you have been promised.

Chapter Seventeen

THE WRITER'S MAGIC

X Is to Mind as Mind to Body

Let us pretend, for convenience, that this faculty, this genius which is present in all of us to a greater or less degree, has been isolated, analyzed, and studied; and found to stand in relation to the mind as the mind stands to the body. If the word 'genius' is still too magniloquent a word for comfort, if you fear that under a wily guise you are being introduced to a spiritual quality which discomfits you, bear with the notions a little while, and call the faculty under consideration just ordinary X. Now X is to be thought of like a factor in an algebraic equation – X : Mind :: Mind : Body. In order to think intensively you hold your body still; at the most you engage it in some light, mechanical task which you can carry on like an automaton. To get X into action, then, you must quiet the mind.

This, you will observe, is exactly what those

rhythmical, monotonous, wordless activities had as their obscure end: they were designed to hold mind as well as body in a kind of suspension while the higher, or deeper, faculty was at work. Insofar as they were successful, they were adopted and used over and over. But they are usually awkward, unsatisfactory, and not always uniform in their results. Moreover, they usually take far more time than the unknown quality needs to fulfill its functions. So, if you are fortunate enough to be a young writer who has not yet found a formula for that gestation period of the story, you are in a position to learn a quicker and better way to attain the same end.

Hold Your Mind Still

It is, in short, this: *learn to hold your mind as still as your body*.

For some this advice is so easy to take that they cannot believe anyone has difficulty in following it. If you belong to that happy group, do not try any of the more intensive exercises that follow. You do not need them, and they will only confuse you. But as you come to this spot in the book, close the book over your finger and shut your eyes, holding your mind, for only a few seconds, as still as you can.

Were you successful – even if for only a fraction of a moment? If you have never tried it before, you may be surprised and confounded to find how busy, fluttering, and restless your mind seems. 'The chattering monkey,' an Indian will say of his mind, half in scorn, half in indulgence; much as St. Francis of Assisi called his body, 'My Brother, the Ass.' 'It skitters around like a water bug!' one experimenter exclaimed, in surprise. But it will stop skittering for you, after a little practice; at least it will be still enough to suit your purposes.

Practice In Control

The best practice is to repeat this procedure once a day for several days. Simply close your eyes with the idea of holding your mind quite steady, but feeling no urgency or tension about it. Once a day; don't push it or attempt to force it. As you begin to get results, make the period a little longer, but never strain at it.

If you discover that you cannot learn to do it so easily, try this way: Choose a simple object, like a child's gray rubber ball. (It is better not to select anything with a bright surface or a decided highlight.) Hold the ball in your hand and look at it, confining your attention to that one simple object, and calling your mind back to it quietly whenever it begins to wander. When you are able to think of the object and nothing else for some moments, take the next step. Close your eyes and *go on looking at the ball*, thinking of nothing else. Then see if you can let even that simple idea slip away.

The last method is to let your mind skitter all it pleases, watching it indulgently as it moves. Presently it will grow quieter. Don't hurry it. If it will not be entirely quiet, it will probably be still enough.

The Story Idea as the Object

When you have succeeded, even a little, try holding a story idea, or a character, in your mind, and letting your stillness center around that. Presently you will see the almost incredible results. Ideas which you held rather academically and unconvincingly will take on color and form; a character that was a puppet will move and breathe. Consciously or unconsciously every successful writer who ever lived calls on this faculty to put the breath of life into his creations.

Now you are ready to try the process in more extended form.

The Magic in Operation

Since this is practice work only (although more may come of the ideas you practice on than you expect) you may go at it rather mechanically. Choose any story idea at random. If you do not like to use one of your own cherished plots for this, here is a variation that will work as well: replace the character of a well-known book by someone you know in real life. If your sister had played the role of Becky Sharp, for example, what course would *Vanity Fair* have had to follow? Suppose Gulliver had been a woman? How vague, stiff, or incomplete the idea is, is of no importance. For our purposes, the less satisfactory it seems at the moment the more complete the demonstration of the method's effectiveness. Make a rough outline of the story. Decide on the main characters, then the secondary characters. See as plainly as possible what crucial situation you would like to put them into, and how you would like to leave them at the end. Don't worry about getting them either in or out of their dilemma; simply see them in it, and then see it resolved. Remember here the circle-and-ring experiment, and that envisaging the end was enough to set the means in motion. Think over the whole story in a sort of pleasant, indulgent mood, correcting any obvious absurdities, reminding yourself of this or that item which you would like to include if it could be brought in naturally.

Now take that rough draft of a story out for a walk with you. You are going to walk till you are just mildly tired, and at that time you should be back at your starting place; gauge your distance by that. Get into a smooth and easy swing, not vigorous and athletic – a lazy, loafing walk is better at first, although it may become more rapid later. Now think about your story; let yourself be engrossed in it – but think of it *as a story*, not of how you are going to write it, or what means you will use to get this or that effect. Refuse to let yourself be diverted by anything outside. As you circle back to your starting place, think of the story's end, as though you were laying it aside after reading it.

Inducing the 'Artistic Coma'

Now bathe, still thinking of it in a desultory way, and then go into a dim room. Lie down, flat on your back; the alternative position, to be chosen only if you find that the other makes you too drowsy, is to sit not quite fully relaxed in a low, large chair. When you have taken a comfortable position, do not move again: make your body quiet. Then quiet your mind. Lie there, not quite asleep, not quite awake.

After a while – it may be twenty minutes, it may be an hour, it may be two – you will feel a definite impulse to rise, a kind of surge of energy. Obey it at once; you will be in a slightly somnambulistic state indifferent to everything on earth except what you are about to write; dull to all the outer world but vividly alive to the world of your imagination. Get up and go to your paper or typewriter, and begin to write. The state you are in at that moment is the state an artist works in.

Valedictory

How good a piece of work emerges depends on you and your life: how sensitive, how discriminating you are, how closely your experience reflects the experience of your potential readers, how thoroughly you have taught yourself the elements of good prose writing, how good an ear you have for rhythm. But, limited or not, you will find, if you have followed the exercises, that you can bring forth a shapely, integrated piece of work by this method. It will have flaws, no doubt; but you will be able to see them objectively and work on eradicating them. By these exercises you have made yourself into a good instrument for the use of your own genius. You are flexible and sturdy, like a good tool. You know what it feels like to work as an artist.

Now read all the technical books on the writing of fiction that you can find. You are at last in a position to have them do you some good.

IN CONCLUSION:
SOME PROSAIC POINTERS

Typewriting

As soon as you can, learn to typewrite. Then, if possible, learn to compose on the typewriter. Unless you write very rapidly and plainly, a first draft written by hand is usually one long waste motion. But be sure that you are sacrificing nothing in making the shift from handwriting to writing on a machine. There are persons who are never able to get the same qualities in the machine-written work which they can catch by the more leisurely method. Write two rather similar ideas, one by each method, compare the two. If the typewritten draft is more abrupt, if you find that ideas escape you there which are found in your handwritten draft, composing at the typewriter is not your proper method.

Have Two Typewriters

The professional writer should have two typewriters, a standard machine and a portable – preferably a noiseless portable. Choose machines with the same typeface; they should both be pica, or both be elite. This will enable you to write at your own convenience, in any room, at any free moment, or when traveling. And you can also leave an incomplete piece of work in the machine, as a mute reproach – if you find you need that.

Stationery

Raid a stationery store. There are innumerable pencils on the market, of all grades of softness and several colors. Try them all; you may find the ideal pencil for your purposes. A medium-soft lead is best for most writers: the pages do not smudge, yet no particular pressure is necessary when writing.

Try bond paper and 'laid' paper – paper with a sleek, smooth finish. Many amateurs use a bond paper because they have never had the good fortune to find the smoother finish, yet the grain in a bond paper may irritate them like the feeling of painted china.

Try writing on loose paper, on pads of various sizes, and in notebooks. Have a notebook full of fresh sheets ready to take on any short journey. On a long journey carry typewriter paper and a portable machine, and make the most of your time.

Don't buy the heaviest and most impressive grade of bond paper for your finished manuscripts. It makes too bulky and heavy a package, and the paper shows wear more quickly than the less expensive grades. 'A good sixteen-pound paper,' is the way to ask for what you need. If the clerk doesn't understand you, find a better stationery store.

At the Typewriter: WRITE!

Teach yourself as soon as possible to work the moment you sit down to a machine, or settle yourself with pad and pencil. If you find yourself dreaming there, or biting your pencil end, get up and go to the farthest corner of the room. Stay there while you are getting up steam. When you have your first sentence ready, go back to your tools. If you steadily refuse to lose yourself in reverie at your worktable, you will be rewarded by finding that merely taking your seat there will be enough to make your writing flow.

If you are unable to finish a piece of work at one sitting, make an engagement with yourself to resume work *before you rise from the table.* You will find that this acts like a posthypnotic suggestion, in more ways than one. You will get back to the work without delay, and you will pick up the same note with little difficulty, so that your story will not show as many different styles as a patchwork quilt when it is done.

For Coffee Addicts

If you have an ingrained habit of putting off everything until after you have had your morning coffee, buy a thermos bottle and fill it at night. This will thwart your wily unconscious in the neatest fashion. You will have no excuse to postpone work while you wait for your stimulant.

Coffee Versus Maté

If you tend to drink a great deal of coffee when in the throes of composition, try replacing half of it by maté, a South American drink much like tea, but stimulating and innocuous. It can be bought at any large grocer's, and is very easy to prepare.

Reading

If you are writing a manuscript so long that the prospect of not reading at all until you have finished is too intolerable, be sure to choose books which are as unlike your own work as possible: read technical books, history, or, best of all, books in other languages.

Book and Magazine Buying

Have periodical debauches of book-buying and magazine-buying, and try to formulate to yourself the editor's possible requirements from the type of periodical he issues. Buy a good handbook on fiction markets, and whenever you find an editor asking for manuscripts which sound like the type you are interested in writing, send for a copy of the magazine if you cannot buy it nearer home.

BIBLIOGRAPHY

Edith Wharton, *The Writing of Fiction*, Scribner, 1925.

A. Quiller-Couch, *On the Art of Writing*, Putnam, 1916.

A.Quiller-Couch, *On the Art of Reading*, Putnam, 1920.

Percy Lubbock, *The Craft of Fiction*, Scribner, 1921.

E. M. Forster, *Aspects of the Novel*, Harcourt, Brace, 1927.

The Novels of Henry James, Definitive Edition, Scribner, 1917. In particular, see Preface to *The Ivory Tower*.

Graham Wallas, *The Art of Thought*, Harcourt, Brace, 1926.

Mary Austin, *Everyman's Genius*, Bobbs Merrill, 1925.

Thomas Uzzell, *Narrative Technique*, Harcourt, Brace, 1923.

F. W. H. Myers, *Human Personality and its Survival of Bodily Death*, Longmans, Green, 1920. In particular see the chapter on Genius.

Edith Wharton, 'The Confessions of a Novelist.' *Atlantic Monthly*, April, 1933.

Percy Marks, *The Craft of Writing*, Harcourt. Brace, 1932.

S. T. Coleridge, *Biographia Literaria*. Various editions. Con-

versations of Eckermann with Goethe, tr. by John Oxenford, Dutton, 1931.

Longinus, *On the Sublime*, tr. by W. Rhys Roberts, Macmillan, 1930.

Alexander Pope, *Essay on Criticism*. Various editions.

William Archer, *Play-Making*, Dodd, Mead, 1912.

George Saintsbury, *History of English Prose Rhythm*, Macmillan, 1922.

Charles Williams, *The English Poetic Mind*, Oxford, 1932.

Anonymous, *The Literary Spotlight*, Doran.

24 English Authors, *Mr Fothergill's Plot*, Oxford, 1931.

Douglas Bement, *Weaving the Short Story*, Richard R. Smith, 1931.

Ford Madox Ford, *It Was the Nightingale*, Lippincott, 1933.

Arnold Bennett, *How to Live on 24 Hours a Day*, Doran, 1910.

T. S. Eliot, *Selected Essays*, Harcourt, Brace, 1932.

Virginia Woolf, *The Common Reader*, Harcourt, Brace, 1925.

Virginia Woolf, *Monday or Tuesday*, Harcourt, Brace, 1921.

The Journals of Katherine Mansfield, edited by J. Middleton Murry, Knopf, 1927.

Storm Jameson, *The Georgian Novel and Mr. Robinson*, Morrow, 1929.

Blanche Colton Williams, *Handbook on Story Writing*, Dodd, Mead, 1930.

Henry Seidel Canby, *Better Writing*, Harcourt, Brace, 1926.

Paul Elmer More, *The Shelburne Essays*, 11 vols., Houghton Mifflin.

Irving Babbitt, *The New Laokoon*, Houghton Mifflin, 1910.

Lafcadio Hearn, *Talks to Writers*, Dodd, Mead, 1920.

And, finally, those who read French will treble the number of these books by the works of Sainte-Beuve, Remy de Gourmont, Gustave Flaubert, the Journals of the brothers Goncourt, Jules Lemaître, Paul Valéry, André Gide (see particularly *Les Faux-Monnayeurs*, or the excellent English translation, published in this country under the title *The Counterfeiters*, Knopf, 1927).

– INDEX –

All Pan Books are available at your local bookshop or newsagent, or can be ordered direct from the publisher. Indicate the number of copies required and fill in the form below.

Send to: Macmillan General Books C.S.
                Book Service By Post
                PO Box 29, Douglas I-O-M
                IM99 1BQ

or phone: 01624 675137, quoting title, author and credit card number.

or fax: 01624 670923, quoting title, author, and credit card number.

or Internet: http://www.bookpost.co.uk

Please enclose a remittance* to the value of the cover price plus 75 pence per book for post and packing. Overseas customers please allow £1.00 per copy for post and packing.

*Payment may be made in sterling by UK personal cheque, Eurocheque, postal order, sterling draft or international money order, made payable to Book Service By Post.

Alternatively by Access/Visa/MasterCard

Card No. ☐☐☐☐☐☐☐☐☐☐☐☐☐☐☐☐

Expiry Date ☐☐☐☐☐☐☐☐☐☐☐☐☐☐☐☐

Signature _____

Applicable only in the UK and BFPO addresses.

While every effort is made to keep prices low, it is sometimes necessary to increase prices at short notice. Pan Books reserve the right to show on covers and charge new retail prices which may differ from those advertised in the text or elsewhere.

NAME AND ADDRESS IN BLOCK CAPITAL LETTERS PLEASE

Name _____

Address _____

_____

_____

_____

8/95

Please allow 28 days for delivery.
Please tick box if you do not wish to receive any additional information. ☐